GOULD'S GOLD AND SILVER GUIDE TO COINS

GOULD'S GOLD AND SILVER GUIDE TO COINS

Maurice M. Gould

FLEET PRESS CORPORATION
New York

© *Copyright* 1969 FLEET PRESS CORPORATION

All Rights Reserved

Library of Congress Catalogue Card Number:
70-76025

No portion of this book may be reprinted in any form without the written permission of the publisher, except by a reviewer who wishes to quote brief passages in connection with a review for a newspaper, magazine, or radio-television program.

Manufactured in the United States of America.

DEDICATION

This volume is dedicated to my beloved daughter, Debbie Jane, who loved the Beatles, and collected their records along with her coins. She thrilled to the search of scarce coins, and was delighted when she could present them to her dad.

ACKNOWLEDGMENTS

There are many who have helped me over the years with their interesting stories and facts and their enthusiasm for the wonderful hobby of coin collecting.

I am indebted to Leonard Finn, Frank Washburn, Howard Gibbs, Major Sheldon S. Carroll, and the numerous numismatists and friends whom I have met at coin clubs and conventions throughout the United States and Canada.

Without the hard work of my wife, Jean, this book could never have become a reality, and I owe her special thanks for her perseverance and loyalty.

Dr. S. George Little, my mentor in the syndicated column field, gave me encouragement and assistance from the very beginning. My warm personal thanks to him.

The year 1968 marks the anniversary of my 50th year in numismatics. This long association with the numismatic hobby has proved fruitful to me both in friends and enduring pleasure for many years.

The hobby of coin collecting, which goes back to the days of the ancients, has grown in stature and has matured during the past ten years.

The hobby of kings is now known as the "king of hobbies."

Maurice M. Gould

March, 1969
Sherman Oaks, California

CONTENTS

I	A Century of Coin Collecting and a Look at some Numismatic Rarities	11
II	Of Doubloons, Pieces of Eight and Buried Treasure	35
III	Putting Your Dollars in Coins—Numismatics for Investment and Speculation	48
IV	A Guide for the New Numismatist	70
V	Hawaiian Scrip, Alaskan Bingles and Puerto Rican Clay Faces	85
VI	Some Numismatic Stores—The Coin Spins a Tale	115
VII	The Interesting World of the Exonumist	140
VIII	Colonial Hog Money, Pine Trees and Bungtown Coppers	161
IX	Numismatics of our Neighbor to the North	171
X	The Royal Metal of Numismatics	182
XI	Some Questions and Answers from the Coin Collector's Mailbag	192
XII	Coin Values for the Collector and Investor	216
XIII	Coins of Israel	250

A Century of Coin Collecting and a Look at Some Numismatic Rarities

The "King of Hobbies" or the "Hobby of Kings" is a pastime almost as old as history itself.

Coin collecting, or *numismatics,* can be traced back to the ancient Greek and Roman periods. Archaelogical excavations have unearthed ancient coins in the finest state of preservation from collections that obviously included coins from each part of the then known world. From early times to the present day, this great and exciting hobby has stirred the imaginations of young and old.

Some European universities—notably in Hamburg and in Vienna—maintained Chairs in numismatics many years ago and the study of ancient and medieval coins and their relation to history and economies was widely explored.

The famous Rothschild fortune had its humble beginning in numismatics. Mayer Rothschild was in a second-hand furniture and minor antique business, but he had always been

Coin of Cleopatra, 51-30 B.C. issued shortly before her death.

interested in old coins and eventually added to his established business a new department for the trading of old coins.

Rothschild would buy all of the old coins that were available to him, study them eagerly and classify them. From his love of numismatics a business developed that led to the sale of a handful of his rarest medals and coins to His Highness, Prince William of Hesse-Hanau. Rothschild acquired other coin collections and soon numbered Duke Karl August of Weimar and other noblemen among his new customers. He started issuing elaborately hand written catalogs with excellent, lovingly phrased descriptions that appealed to his customers.

Prince William subsequently appointed Rothschild a Court Factor, and thus it was that Mayer Rothschild's interest in numismatics led to the family's power in international finance and to Rothschild becoming personal banker to kings and emperors.

* * *

Because of the tremendous rise in prices during the last decade, there are many coins which are now worth $10,000 or more each. On the following pages, you will learn of exciting and highly publicized numismatic treasures which *you* may one day be able to add to *your* coin collection.

The 1913 *Liberty Head Nickel* (5 known)

Always mentioned with awe and reverence by the collector is the 1913 Liberty Head nickel, and yet like the 1804 Silver Dollar and other sought-for rarities, this piece has been the subject of controversial discussion that will probably never be resolved.

The five pieces now known have an interesting and documented history, going back to Samuel Brown of North Tonawanda, New York, who first offered these pieces for sale. They were acquired by Colonel E.H.R. Green of New Bedford, Massachusetts, the son of the fabulous Hetty Green, one of the world's wealthiest women. Colonel Green, who devoted a great deal of time to numerous hobbies, was a particularly avid collector of stamps and coins, often purchasing entire collections just to acquire a single piece that he really wanted. Colonel Green employed one secretary just to handle the correspondence and cataloguing of his coin and stamp inventory. The Colonel took substantial pride in his ownership of all five 1913 Liberty Head Nickels and placed advertisements offering $50 each for additional examples of this piece. These offers, however, were really only a conceit as there were no other 1913 Liberty Heads available.

When Colonel Green died, the 1913 Liberty Head nickels were sold at auction for $800. each and ultimately became a part of some of the world's most important collections, including that of Egypt's King Farouk.

For years one of America's top coin dealers offered to purchase 1913 Liberty Head nickels for $50. each. Actually he would have been quite safe to have offered $10,000. each, for there were simply none available. But he kept millions of Americans looking anxiously for this elusive piece by creating the impression that some might still be found in circulation. Most of the avid "lookers" came up with the Buffalo Nickel, which was first issued in 1913, and was quite common.

In spite of the contrast between the rumors and authentic information known about this much-discussed coin, it probably will always be sought for because it is one of the glamour coins of U.S. collecting.

At a West Coast auction in 1961, a 1913 Liberty Nickel received a bid of $41,000, but was not sold as the owner wanted at least $50,000 for it.

1894-S Dime, (24 Coined)

Among the most sought and often described United States coins is the 1894 San Francisco Mint dime.

With only twenty-four specimens struck, this coin naturally creates excitement and breaks price records whenever it is offered for sale. Most of the specimens in museums and private collections are in uncirculated or "mint" condition, but there is one specimen that got into circulation somehow and is classed as only in "Good to Very Good" condition.

A great deal of argument has been advanced that the 1894 San Francisco dime was a *pièce de caprice,* but the fact that one specimen did get into circulation indicates that these coins might have been struck with larger numbers to be coined eventually.

If these twenty-four pieces actually were struck for circulation, then the 1894 San Francisco dime had the smallest minting of any United States date or mintmark coined for this purpose.

At a public auction in 1961, the Hydeman specimen brought $13,000 and since then, there have been offers in excess of $20,000 made for this coin. Because of its extreme rarity the 1894 San Francisco dime is seldom offered for sale and bidding is always brisk when it is available at auction.

Such a coin might be compared in value to a Van Gogh, Rubens, Titian, or other modern or old master paintings, and will always be in demand with probable sensational increases in value.

The Most Popular United States Small Cent (approximately 1,000 coined)

The most glamourous United States cent is the 1856 *Flying Eagle cent.*

This coin was not an authorized issue and is actually a *pattern coin* or *trial piece.* It is estimated that approximately 1,000 of these pieces were struck. Actually this coin is not a required piece in a regular U.S. set by dates, but manufacturers of coin supplies always included this date in the coin holders and naturally, everyone wanted this date to complete his set. This coin catalogs from $650 for pieces in "Good" condition, to $2,850 for "Proof" condition examples. It comes in a number of different metals besides the regular copper-nickel coinage and the variations are more valuable.

There are many altered dates and other imitations on the market and extreme caution should be used in purchasing this coin at a bargain price or from anyone you do not know to be reputable. In coin collecting the phrase "know your dealer" is

United States Flying Eagle Cent

of vital importance. Over the years, in looking through many collections, I have found many of these coins thought by their owners to be genuine which were actually electrotypes, cast pieces, altered dates, etc.

There is one large hoard of close to 400 pieces which has been in a vault in Pennsylvania since the 1890's, due to litigation among the heirs of a large estate. What would happen if these were all released at the same time? It would be very interesting to see how fast these would be absorbed into collections and by dealers.

At one time I owned an 1856 Flying Eagle cent that came in a small envelope across the face of which was written in longhand,

> "Presented to my faithful bodyservant,
> Pres. James Buchanan."

The 1856 Flying Eagle cent will always be in demand and will create excitement whenever it is displayed or offered for sale.

During the 1940's, one of the country's leading coin dealers was just about ready to close his place of business for the evening when a gentleman came in with two coins for sale.

Both of these pieces were the rare and much sought-after 1856 Flying Eagle cent.

The seller wanted $45 for one and $75 for the other. Although they were very desirable, this was a rather large sum of money for a coin dealer to invest at that time. He could not afford to purchase both, so he astutely decided to buy the better one at $75. In order to pay for it, he had to turn in many silver coins, some worth even more than face value. He then closed up shop and went home.

On arriving at his house he was told that his wife had been rushed to the hospital, and within the space of a short time, he was notified that his wife had given birth to a baby girl.

He told his wife how he had purchased the 1856 Flying Eagle cent that day, and they decided to name their daughter Penny.

Eventually, Penny was married, and her dowry was the same 1856 Flying Eagle cent that her father had purchased at great sacrifice twenty years before. This rare coin has now appreciated to a value of several thousand dollars—a dowry appreciated by any bride.

This story points up a basic maxim for coin collectors. When you believe and have faith in a coin, don't let it slip by, but purchase it, enjoy it, and eventually your faith, coupled with knowledge, will pay great dividends in both pleasure and financial gain.

I recently spoke with this dealer and he said that he is still looking for 1856 Flying Eagle cents, even though he can no longer purchase them at the price he did twenty years ago, but if one is available at a reasonable price, he will purchase it to set aside for his first grandchild.

The 1864-L *Indian Head Cent*

One of the most sought after Indian head cents is the one dated 1864 with the L on the ribbon.

The coin without the L is fairly common and the mintage is a little over 39,000,000. Probably included in this figure is the 1864 with L because no records have been found showing the number struck of this variety.

The initial is that of J. B. Longacre, the mint engraver of this period. It is interesting to note that all Indian head cents dated after 1864 do have the L.

The simplest way that I know to locate the L is to place the obverse of the coin before you with the words "of America" directly in front of you. Look at the word "Liberty" and go along following the line of this word. The "L" appears underneath the last feather and is slightly raised.

Another method of checking the "L" on the ribbon is to look at the extreme lower left of the Indian head cent. If it is the "L" the bust will be pointed and just over the "1" in the date. If it is the plain 1864, it is round and extends far over the "1" in the date.

In spite of the fact that I have read stories to the contrary, there are cases where the "L" can be seen in coins which may be only Fair or Good condition, but naturally the better the condition, the stronger the "L" shows up.

The 1864-L catalogs $50 in Fine condition and $225 in Uncirculated condition and is worth several thousand dollars in Proof condition for there are only 20 specimens known.

The 1868 *Large Cent*

One of the most unusual coins I have ever owned was the 1868 U.S. large cent. I purchased this piece many years ago because it looked exactly like a large cent, although it was dated eleven years *after* the last large cents were struck and when Indian Head cents were being issued annually. It always

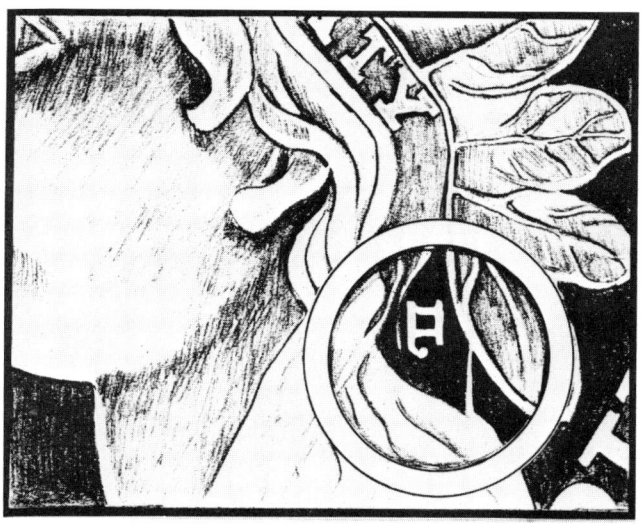

Circle shows location of the "L" on the 1864 Indian Head cent. New collectors find it difficult to locate this mark.

attracted a great deal of interest and aroused controversy whenever I would show it.

Probably this piece was struck by mint employees during the period when special pieces like the 1884 and 1885 Trade Dollars and similar items were struck especially for a collector who had friends or contacts at the Mint.

There are only a few pieces known of the 1868 large cent and the rise in value can be gauged by comparing my purchase price of $50, which in 1945, I thought to be a considerable amount, to the $1200 I received for it at the 1960 American Numismatic Association Convention. I have recently seen the piece advertised at more than $7,000.

A coin such as this proves that no matter what its background, if a collector wants a particular coin, he is willing to pay for it, and of course, the more unobtainable an item is, the more collectors are looking for it.

U.S. Colonial Coin Rarities

Among the rare American Colonial items is the *New England 3 pence* of which only two pieces are known. A crude striking with "N.E." on the obverse and the denomination on the reverse, these pieces were used for only a short period.

Another important rarity is the *Willow Tree 3 pence* of which only three pieces are known.

It is difficult to even estimate values on most of these early Colonial rarities since they are so seldom offered at private sale or auction that an estimated value would be little more than a wild guess. From $1,000 for some of the lesser rarities up to $50,000 perhaps for the famous Brasher Doubloon should suggest the incredible price range.

Massachusetts Pine Tree Copper, 1776

This coin is said to have been designed by Paul Revere and is unique.

All new Hampshire Colonial pieces are rare to extremely rare and are seldom seen in any collection.

The *Vermont cent,* dated 1787, with the bust left, is another rare piece and the 1787 *New York cent* with a large eagle on the reverse and arrows and branch transposed, are equally rare.

Massachusetts issued the 1776 *Pine Tree cent,* the 1776 *Janus Copper,* both of which are said to be unique.

Some varieties of the *Continental Dollar* and all of the *Nova Constellatio Silver Pattern* are on almost every want list.

The *Nova Constellatio Copper,* dated 1786, is another great rarity of which one piece was recently found in Maine.

The historic *Brasher Doubloon* is of the greatest rarity. This well-known coin has been publicized on television and in the movies alike.

Varieties of the *Higley-Connecticut Coppers* of 1737 are among the top rarities and the 1694 *God Preserve New England* as well as the 1694 *Proprieters* are other rarities.

The *Virginia Silver shilling* of 1774, the *New England Stiver,* and genuine *Castorland* pieces are among the most difficult coins to obtain, as are pieces among the *Fugio cents* and the *Washington tokens.*

The first United States Mint issues are all "Rare" to "Unique." Included among these are the *disme,* dated 1792, in silver, of which only three pieces are known.

The 1792 *Copper ½ disme* is unique. The 1792 *Birch cent* is a remarkably elusive coin.

There is also a 1792 *cent,* one which has no silver center and another piece that does have one. These were trial pieces to determine which form would be best for wear. Along with the 1792 *Pattern ½ Eagle,* these pieces round out items of early American coinage that are most difficult to obtain.

$3 *Gold Piece*

With the exception of a few years, the $3 gold pieces issued from 1854 to 1889 in very small numbers are all scarce or rare.

The largest mintage was 138, 618 in 1854 and the smallest mintage was 20 pieces struck in 1875, making this the rarest $3 gold piece.

Naturally, some of these pieces are in museums. A few may

Fugio Cent
Reverse of famous United States Colonial coin

possibly have been destroyed.

When one of the 1875 $3 gold pieces was offered at auction at the Wolfson sale in October, 1962 it brought $17,000. Some owners have valued their pieces at $25,000.

The 1876 piece, is also extremely valuable. One of these pieces brought $8,100. at an auction in 1963. It may be years before a piece of this calibre will be available again.

$4 *Gold Piece*

Outside of the numismatic specialist very few people have heard of a U.S. $4 gold piece, which has the delightful nickname of "Stella."

1792 Half-Disme
One of the first United States Mint Issues. These pieces were made from Martha Washington's silver plate.

Issued in extremely small numbers for two years the $4 gold piece has two different types—the "Flowing Hair" and "Coiled Hair."

They were struck in four metals: gold, aluminum, copper, and white metal, but the gold is in greatest demand since this coin would have been a $4 gold piece if it had been accepted by the government for use in circulation.

The largest number struck was 415 pieces of the 1879 "Flowing Hair" with a catalog value of $6,000. The other pieces in gold catalog from $12,000 to $15,000.

This series is classed in the pattern category and seldom is seen except in museums or in the most advanced collections.

The Unique English Penny of 1954

Do you have a 1954 English penny? This coin is worth thousands of dollars, but do not bother to look for it as the piece

1792 Silver Center Cent
This Colonial piece is so rare that it is unpriced in the catalog and is rarely offered for sale.

is Unique. There is no chance of finding another one.

This rare coin was brought from England in 1964 by a coin dealer in upstate New York. It has been on exhibition at a number of conventions. It came from the famous collection of C. Wilson Peck, well-known numismatic author and collector.

A very small number of English pennies were struck in 1954 at the Royal Mint in London, but when no further orders came for coins of this denomination, the dies, along with the coins, were destroyed, except for the one coin that was acquired in 1956 by an English dealer, who eventually sold it to Mr. Peck for his collection of British coins.

Mr. Peck considered this piece the outstanding one in his famous collection. He never exhibited the coin publicly and it was only known through information listed in the British Museum catalog in which it was also pictured.

This 1954 English Penny will always be a great rarity as it is wanted by both museums and collectors on both sides of the Atlantic, and naturally, many Englishmen would be delighted to have it back on British soil.

Rarity is obviously not dependent upon age, for this coin, only recently minted, would bring a fabulous price at any auction or private sale.

Canadian Gold Rarity

The 1918-C *Mint sovereign* is one of the great rarities in Canadian coins.

Specimens have changed hands for prices varying from $15,000 to $30,000.

As with many other rarities, there is a mystery attached to this coin. The records at the Ottawa Mint show that 6,111 pieces were struck, though few have found their way into museum or private collections, making this one of the most desirable of modern gold pieces.

It is of course possible that pieces still may be in the vaults of some bank or banking house, even though collectors and research students have made every effort to locate them.

A specimen from the stock of a well-known Canadian dealer was sent to the Royal Mint for examination to authenticate the coin's genuineness and the conclusion was that the coin was genuine in every respect.

Perhaps more information will come to light as a result of the great amount of research being done. It might reveal some fascinating story about the "Queen of Canadian Gold Pieces."

Konstantine Rouble of 1825

Although little known in the United States, this *Russian crown* became one of the world's most famous silver coins, when it was offered at a New York auction in November, 1965, at an estimated value of $41,000.

An interesting bit of history accounts for the rarity of this piece. Next in line to the throne held by his brother, Czar Alexander I, Konstantine had divorced the Princess Juliana of Saxe-Coburg, and married the Polish Countess Johanna Grudzinska.

It had been suggested many times that portraits of the Czars appear on the coinage, but for one reason or another, this had not been done before.

Upon the death of Alexander I, Konstantine immediately renounced his right to succession in favor of his younger brother, Nicholas I.

It was at this time however that the Petersburg Mint, in preparing new dies and coinage for the Czar, engraved dies bearing the portrait of Konstantine.

Although dies already had been completed and tested, the royal family ordered the pieces to be shipped to the Ministry of Finance and placed in the secret archives. Included in the shipment were five pattern coins struck from these dies.

The engraver of the dies, J. Reichel, a well-known coin

collector, had a specimen of the coin struck for himself before the dies had been stored, for he could not resist the opportunity to add one of these rarities to his famous collection. His coin however is distinguished from the other pieces in that it does not have a lettered edge.

Naturally, Reichel tried to keep his possession of the Konstantine rouble a secret, but through showing the piece or bragging of it to other collectors, the existence of the mysterious and exciting coin became known.

Minister of Finance, E. F. Kankrin, then thought it best to circulate a rumor that the coins and dies were destroyed, except for three pieces that had been deliverd to Konstantine in Poland.

Eventually, the famous Reichel collection was acquired by the Hermitage Museum in Leningrad, which houses one of the world's greatest coin collections.

Over the years, stories and rumors concerning the Konstantine roubles have mushroomed until it is extremely difficult to sift the truth from the varied assortment of rumor and conjecture.

One story goes that in the 1870's Trubetzkoi, a former army officer, persuaded a Mr. Girault, a coin dealer who represented a wealthy American collector named Webster, to buy the five coins.

Girault is said to have disappeared in the wreck of the ship, "City of Boston," in 1870. With him was lost Webster's luggage, purportedly containing the coins.

Over the years, unsuccessful attempts to authenticate various aspects of the story have been made, and for a time, the Konstantine rouble became an object of bitter dispute involving charges of misrepresentation and fraud. Then in 1880 the Chief of Chancery at the Ministry of Finance, D. F. Kobeko, who had access to the records and who also happened to be a coin collector, published the facts from the Archives of the Ministry, along with the contents of the documents of 1825, establishing the authenticity of the dies and coins.

In 1879, Czar Alexander II confiscated the coins from the Ministry. He donated one piece to the Hermitage Museum, kept one for himself, and gave the remaining three to members of the royal family—the Grand Dukes Georgii Mikhailovitch, Sergei Alexandrowitch, and Prince Alexander of Hesse.

The coins have since been in numerous hands, but are, at least, pedigreed. The piece that was in the United States belonged to one of the most famous American collectors, Virgil M. Brand. After Brand's death in 1926, it remained with his family until 1964, when it was sold for $11,650 at an auction in Lucerne, Switzerland.

The Konstantine rouble, with its intriguing and mysterious history, could easily be incorporated into a contemporary "cloak and dagger" adventure were all its fascinating story known.

100 Years of Coin Collecting in the U.S.

During the 1860's, coin collecting, as it is practiced today, had its real inception. Before that time, there were, of course, isolated enthusiasts and collectors, but there were no numismatic organizations or clubs, no research, and no reference works available to the students.

About the middle of the nineteenth century, numismatic literature began to appear. In one early work, "Coins, Medals and Seals,"[1] by W. C. Prime, the author states:

> "It is impossible to affirm in this day whether certain coins now very rare will remain so since every year new specimens of rare coins are found and added to collections. For this reason the price catalogs are of only temporary value, so, too, with the silver of the years preceding 1853. For the present, most of the dates can be readily obtained; but in consequence of the change in weight which took

---

1. W. C. Prime Coins, Medals and Seals, Harper & Bros., New York, 1864.

place in 1853, the silver of earlier date than that has almost entirely disappeared from circulation and is now sold to the melters or returned to the mint. As this practice continues, the entire early coinage is becoming scarce, so that within a year from the present time, many half-dollars, quarters, dimes, and half-dimes, now common, will become of the highest rarity and command the highest prices." [*Similar cirumstances prevailed in* 1964 *when the silver nickels of the war years,* 1942 *through '45, were melted for their silver value, and also because of the need for more silver* — M.M.G.]

"Tradesmen's cards, tokens, and medalets of all kinds have for the same reason no fixed value or steadfast price in any scale of rarity. The mania, no other word can be correctly used, which during the past year, has led to the payment of enormous prices for tradesmen's cards, has received a fitting check by the reproduction in immense quantities from the original dies of many of the most highly prized."

"For this reason it is impossible today to say that any one card or token will be scarce or especially valuable tomorrow."

"At present the science of numismatics in America has very few devotees. Collectors we have without number who hunt diligently for tradesmen's cards and mistakes in dies and who collect for a year, then sell their cabinets at auction and begin again, but we have very few students of the science."

The mania for collecting tokens in the 1860's, referred to by Prime, again came to pass in the 1880's. This series has again attracted the attention of collectors in the 1960's.

The restriking of tokens and medals which Prime mentions has also taken place in recent times.

During the early years of U.S. numismatics, ancient and foreign coins were popular items for collection, along with American Colonial coins and currency. The auction records show the high prices that various tokens and medals brought and collecting political tokens was extremely popular.

Lacking accessories that we take for granted today, early numismatists kept their collections in various kinds of cabinets with shallow drawers, usually with a piece of velvet or felt to serve as a bed for the coins. Such arrangements made showing a collection very easy but did not afford the protection modern coin cards offer. Recently, I visited a coin dealer and noticed that he wore a pair of fine white gloves when handling his uncirculated coins, thereby keeping off the moisture and foreign matter which might eventually cause corrosion.

The popularity of coin collecting continued to increase and by the late 1890's, there were enough interested collectors to form the American Numismatic Association (ANA), which today is the world's largest numismatic organization, with a membership of more than 25,000.

Dr. George Francis Heath, who has been termed the "Father of the American Numismatic Association," was the first to suggest organization of an international coin collector's society. It was largely through the untiring efforts of this remarkable man that the organization, once formed, moved steadily forward.

Dr. Heath, who in addition to his prominence in the medical profession, had also served a term as Mayor of the city of Munroe, Michigan, first collected coins in 1863. Ten years later his collection was ruined by a disastrous fire. Heath immediately began collecting again and assembled a very fine collection. While Heath's other hobbies included collecting stamps, autographs, minerals, and Indian relics, coins were foremost in his interest. He started a small coin publication called "The Numismatist." In one of the early issues he asked the question, "Why should there not be an American Numismattic Association?" It was not long thereafter that the ANA came into existence.

Had he so wished, Dr. Heath might have become permanent president of the organization, but he stepped aside and urged Mr. William G. Jerrems, Jr., of Chicago, to accept the position. First place in the ANA, however, should certainly be assigned to its founder, the distinguished numismatist, Dr. George Francis Heath.

First secretary of the ANA was Charles Tatman of Worcester, Massachusetts. Tatman, a well-known tennis enthusiast, became one of the mainstays of the national numismatic organization.

Surviving formative trials and tribulations the ANA has grown and prospered and today has its national headquarters in Colorado Springs, Colorado, where they maintain their own offices, library and museum. The ANA speaks for the world's largest group of true coin collectors.

The popularity of numismatics increased, and in the 1930's, the first manufactured coin folders, or holders, intrigued the public, stimulating still wider interest in coin collecting. Many millions of these boards have been sold, and today coin folders are available in almost all department stores, five-and-tens, greeting card shops—even at some automobile service stations—as well as from coin dealers handling these supplies.

With the distribution of the first cards, millions of coins were taken from circulation to fill out the boards and holders of collectors dates and mintmarks. New collectors from eight to eighty took up the hobby and the number of American numismatists grew to an estimated ten to twelve million collectors.

Another stimulant to collecting was the issuance of a standard coin catalog listing up-to-date values and prices. This annual publication proved helpful to collector and dealer alike. The first catalog issued by Wayte Raymond was followed by the *Whitman Guide Book* which is still revised each year, with new editions and information to keep the collector well informed and up to date.

It was in the late 1950's that a new kind of collector—the investor—came into the numismatic field. Although a few collectors had always put away an occasional roll of coins or a proof set for use in trading or eventual resale at a nominal profit, the new group that came into the coin market was interested in doing business on a large scale. In addition to a great deal of money, they brought experience and techniques developed in other investment markets. A large circulation bimonthly and a weekly newspaper, were printed along with many tipster sheets and investment newspapers.

The coin-collecting boom skyrocketed until whatever one purchased could be sold at a profit within a few days. This situation attracted a large number of fly-by-night speculators, as well as legitimate investors, and the letdown and eventual price leveling-off that started in the summer of 1965 was inevitable.

Foreign proof sets, as well as U.S. proof sets, bags, and rolls of coins enjoyed frequent trading, and when silver dollars were released by the U.S. Treasury, they became still another means of investment. In some cases, investors were forced to turn in some of the late-date United States coins at face value after paying premiums and interest charges on them.

In the 1960's, thousands of coin clubs were formed in the United States and Canada. Coin shows and numismatic conventions increased in frequency until it seemed that there were not enough days in the week on which to attend them and scheduling conflicts became everyday occurrences.

Among the many hundreds of kinds of collecting to be seen at such meetings and exhibits are:

Collecting by periods—only coins from 1800 to 1900, for example.

Collecting by topic—only coins on which animals are represented, for example, or some other subject in which the collector is particularly interested.

Collecting coins of each metal that has been used since coinage began.

Collecting tokens, medals, paper money, even stamps that have coins on them.

One has to be guided by his own personal taste. A specialized collection reaches its peak when displayed properly and often wins prizes at club exhibits and coin shows.

In 1965 the trend in collecting turned to type coins in both the United States and Canadian series. In part, this was attributable to the tremendous increase in prices of regular mintmark and date coins, since the average collector could no longer afford the inflated values.

Foreign coin collecting was starting out on a large scale, with British and Mexican coins as well as the coins of the West Indies and Central America being featured. Many of the foreign pieces are relatively inexpensive in comparison with the U.S. and Canadian coins and this has made them particularly appealing to many beginners, youngsters, and students.

The true collector, in the strict sense of the word, has once again become king and the investor has had to become something of a collector in order to retain some tenure in the hobby.

The imagination is stirred by the sensational rise in prices of coins. A coin that brought $1,000 a number of years ago has skyrocketed in value beyond belief. I was offered one of the 1913 Liberty nickels for $800 a number of years ago and wanted desperately to own one, but the amount asked at that time seemed like a small fortune to me. Now the approximate value of that coin would be $50,000!

The 1804 dollar, with an approximate value of $30,000; the 1894 San Francisco dime, approximately $15,000; and the 1866 quarter and half-dollar, at $40,000 for the pair, are prime examples of the tremendous rise in coin prices. Inexpensive coins have also risen in value, many of them in higher percentage than the more valuable coins.

The old-time coin dealer was usually a student well versed in numismatics, with a large stock of material that he hoped to sell. He usually had plenty of time available for discussions and the dispersion of knowledge.

Today, the coin dealer is often an energetic business man running an efficient business. His stock may turn over several times a year, and his advertising and merchandising is kept up to the minute.

The year 1964 was highlighted with a new slogan, "Education in Numismatics." That slogan has become a byword today.

A few classes in numismatics had been held in various parts of the country, usually with the emphasis on investment and the speculative market. But because of the interest of thousands of new collectors, many regular numismatic classes have been formed. I was instrumental in originating a class held at the Massachusetts Institute of Technology and sponsored by the Massachusetts Department of Education, through the University Extension Division, for which the influx of students was so great that it became necessary to schedule additional classes in order to accomodate the unexpectedly large group.

That year I also conducted numismatic classes at the Boston Center for Adult Education to which many guest lecturers, known for particular specialties, gave informative, and enthusiastically received, talks.

With the backing of the Professional Numismatist Guild, Arthur Kagin of Des Moines, Iowa planned a course in numismatics which was given at the Roosevelt University in Chicago for full credit. Other institutions and coin groups have followed suit until there are now many numismatic classes being conducted throughout the country.

Although this phase of numismatics is still in its infancy, it augurs well for the future to have proper education available to devotees of the hobby.

II

Of Doubloons, Pieces of Eight, and Buried Treasure

One of the great thrills in numismatics is to find a coin —or a hoard—whether through excavation, or at the bottom of the ocean, or in the blackened walls of an ancient chimney.

Coins are constantly being located by archaeologists digging in Europe and the Far East. In areas once occupied by the Romans, pots or vessels filled with ancient coins frequently have been unearthed. During the Second World War the devastating bombings, while irreparably damaging many buildings and antiquities, also brought to light hidden hoards of coins and countless single pieces.

Tons of numismatic treasure—medals, tokens, and coins of all ages, metals, and sizes—have rested for centuries in the ocean. Occasionally an odd piece has been brought in by the tides and washed up on the shores at Plymouth, Massachusetts, or Plymouth, England, at the Cape of Good Hope, or along the coast of Australia.

In recent years, through scientific and technological advances it has been possible to salvage much numismatic treasure from the ocean floor. Many collections have been enriched with pieces bearing hitherto unknown dates and mintmarks, particularly in the Spanish Colonial series.

Oak Island

One of history's most unusual treasure hunts is the Oak Island, Nova Scotia, search which began as far back as 1795 when three boys, enjoying the adventure of exploring on the tiny island, noticed a hole in the earth and started digging.

Since then, there has been a steady procession of owners and treasure hunters exploring everywhere on Oak Island, working to uncover what is believed to be the famous Captain Kidd's buried treasure, with an estimated value of from $100,000,000 to $200,000,000.

There are many legends surrounding Captain Kidd and other pirates believed to have buried treasures in the area. Owners of Oak Island have made numerous studies to find out what is buried there and where.

The three boys who first started digging on Oak Island had come upon an oak platform about ten feet down, and since that platform was found, continuous excavations have unearthed platforms going down to a depth of 9 feet, at ten foot intervals. There have been unconfirmed statements of gold coins and fragments of gold objects being brought to the surface of the so-called "money pit."

When the various levels have been reached, quantities of charcoal, putty, and cocoanut fiber have been brought up and indications are that these were placed there at an earlier period.

One interesting item discovered by the three boys in 1795 was a stone covered with curious symbols that when deciphered, were said to read "10 feet below, 2,000,000 pounds are buried."

The most promising period in the search came in drilling

at 98 feet when a platform was pierced and after going through some empty space, the drill cut into four inches of oak, followed by twenty-two inches of metal pieces, then eight inches of oak and another twenty-two inches of metal. Another four inches of oak followed and six of spruce before the drill hit deep clay. From this it was surmised that there were two treasure chests buried one atop the other, filled with gold coins and jewels. The most exciting item that came to the surface was three links from a gold chain.

The greatest enemy of the treasure hunters has been the sea. Each time it has seemed that excavations might prove fruitful, water has entered the various shafts and tunnels, washing away all work previously accomplished. Over the years the work has taken the lives of many men and cost millions of dollars, yet in spite of the tragedies and heartaches connected with this project, a U.S. geologist has now purchased Oak Island and is following a long-cherished dream of finding the buried treasure. Relying on modern equipment and scientific research, the new owner has devised a secret plan to cut off the water at the beach or to pump it directly out of the excavations.

There seems to be no question that some treasure is buried at Oak Island, but no one yet knows if the dreams of many adventurers will come to a golden fruition or if more and more lives will be lost in the legendary quest.

Texas Treasure

Among the most famous treasures that have ever been sought is the Texas Silver Hoard, said to be worth $2,000,000 and believed to be at the bottom of Hendrick's Lake, 200 miles north of Houston. It is believed that the famous pirate, Jean LaFitte, robbed a Spanish ship, the Santa Rosa, near Galveston, Texas, and made arrangements to ship his treasure to St. Louis for conversion into cash. LaFitte hired an agent who loaded the silver on six mule-drawn wagons to make the northward trip along with his regular freight caravan. When a group of Spanish soldiers cought up with the caravan, most of the members of the party were killed, though a few did manage to escape. The legend goes that the caravan riders dumped the silver into a nearby lake, just before the Spanish attacked.

As early as 1855, an attempt was made to recover the treasure by draining the lake, but heavy rains interfered with the venture. Since then, many groups have attempted to recover the treasure. In the late 1920's, the legend of LaFitte's silver was again revived, when a fisherman hooked onto three silver bars. Several groups, convinced the treasure is still there, have continued to search the lake bottom and are trying to develop electronic detection equipment that will operate properly under water, enabling them to do the necessary work to recover the treasure.

Undoubtedly some of the treasure will eventually be recovered to find its way into museums and the hands of private collectors.

New England's Part in Buried Treasure

Edward Rowe Snow, the eminent marine historian, has researched many pirate treasures, wrecks, etc. and has come up with literally hundreds of facts, as well as legends, concerning New England's fascinating role in these adventures.

It has long been known that one who walks on a New England beach just after a storm is likely to be rewarded by finding one or two silver coins of Spanish origin. Sometimes large amounts are found and even chests of silver and gold have been uncovered.

A hoard of two thousand silver coins was discovered by a lobster fisherman on Haskell Island and a kettle filled with gold was discovered between Reef Ram Island and Elm Island.

In 1849, one of the largest finds ever made in Maine was valued at $700,000, most of it in *pieces of eight* or 8 *reales*.

One interesting story relates to a Spanish galleon that in 1685 was carried ashore on Star Island off the coast of New Hampshire during a violent storm. The vessel, known to have had a tremendous amount of gold coins, silver bullion, and plate on board, was battered to pieces, but residents of the Island salvaged the valuable timber, which they eventually used in the construction of the Gosport Church.

The Fabulous Treasures of the Spanish Conquerors

In April, 1519, the famous Spanish adventurer, Hernando Cortez, landed in Mexico with a contingent of 600 soldiers. Tough leader that he was, Cortez burned his boats to prevent possible desertion or thoughts of turning back from his dreams of conquest. The most amazing part of this conquest was that with a small group of men, he conquered a nation of untold wealth, having an area larger than that of his mother country.

In 1533, Francisco Pizarro finally conquered Peru, after a great many disheartening and fruitless attempts. It was from this area that huge amounts of valuable bullion were sent back to Spain.

Between 1539 and 1543, Hernando De Soto, with approximately 500 men, explored and searched for treasure throughout what is now the Southeastern United States. While this particular expedition did not uncover any wealth, rumors of treasure circulated throughout the Old World. Incredible stories of Indian tribes using common everyday implements made entirely of gold were circulated and between 1520 and 1540, a great many searches were undertaken.

Spain wanted to make certain that the wealth of the New World would be siphoned off to the Spanish treasury. All of the mineral resources of the Spanish Colonies were claimed by the Crown. Individuals working the mines were made to forfeit half or one-third of everything their labors produced, as huge wealth flowed into the Spanish treasuries from the Indian-operated gold and silver mines.

The Spaniards were very systematic about the exploitation of the wealth of the colonies. Fleets of Spanish ships sailed in great numbers twice a year, carrying manufactured goods to the Americas and returning with bullion and raw materials. No other nation was allowed to trade with Spanish America and total economic control was enforced.

Treasure-laden ships would sail from the fortified harbor of Porto Bello, and make the journey to Spain under constant guard. From these treasure-fleets, by violent storms and by pirate attacks, galleons were sent to the bottom of the ocean. Some of the treasure now being recovered from these galleons is of extreme value to numismatists, for hitherto unlisted and unheard-of dates and types have been recovered.

The most famous treasure hunt of recent times took place on Florida's east coast, and among the items brought to the surface were gold coins, still as brilliant as the day they were struck, pieces of eight, as well as ingots of silver and gold.

For years, beachcombers and curiosity seekers have been finding pieces of eight and other coins on the Florida beaches, so it seemed apparent that treasure must lie not far from the coast.

Almost an entire galleon fleet went to the bottom of the ocean in 1715 and it is from these vessels that the Florida treasure is being brought to the surface. More of it will be recovered for many years to come.

The coins which have been brought to the surface were mostly struck at the mint at Mexico City which was of great importance during the early colonial period. The denominations of these hand-hammered pieces are the 4 *reale* and 8 *reale*.

Among the pieces found were gold doubloons which are of great historical and numismatic interest. A doubloon was an important item in the financial transactions of the day and had a purchasing power of several hundred dollars, while the pieces of eight had a value equivalent to ten or fifteen dollars.

Despite being immersed in the ocean for more than two hundred years, the gold that has been brought up is in beautiful condition. On the other hand the silver usually is in deplorable condition.

One of the most unusual items recovered is the remains of a wooden chest filled with silver coins found in the same vessel that had yielded large chunks of silver and individual silver coins. In this instance, a clump of silver coins had adhered to the bottom and sides of the chest and for the first time in this particular search, wood has been brought up along with the silver. The clump of silver was composed of several thousand silver coins fused together through two hundred and fifty years under the sea. This unusual chest has been placed on public display in a Florida museum.

In one area, a thousand gold doubloons was discovered and there is no doubt there are many more still to be found. One group alone has taken over $1,000,000 from the sunken galleons and as more research is done and more expeditions formed to search for the elusive treasures of the Spanish Empire, it is expected that many millions more will be brought to the surface.

The State of Florida, which now shares in any treasure recovered, licenses treasure hunters and carefully watches to see that the state obtains its fair share of any finds.

Dos Mundos

One of the world's best known coins is the famous *Pillar Dollar* or *Dos Mundos* as it is universally called. The mention of these items immediately conjures thoughts of pirates and daring adventure on the high seas.

These are the pieces of eight described by Robert Louis Stevenson in his famous story, *Treasure Island*. No other coin has ever been circulated and accepted in more parts of the world. Only one hundred years ago *Dos Mundos* was legal tender in the United States and passed, current with American coins.

Spanish Colonial Silver (Pirate Money)

When Spain was at its zenith as a colonial power, these coins were minted in great numbers both in Spain and in the Spanish Colonies. The Crown Pillars on the reverse referred to the Pillars of Hercules, now known as the Straits of Gibraltar. The coins were minted from 1732 to 1772 and are universally collected by date and mintmark which makes them increasingly difficult to obtain. Millions of *Dos Mundos* circulated in China even in recent years and many eventually found their way to Hong Kong and have been shipped to the United States in response to the collectors' demands. Unfortunately, most of the pieces coming from China have chopmarks on them. Chopmarks are the small initials or sign of the money changer or broker who checks the coin and certifies that it is of good silver. Some of these coins are so entirely covered with chopmarks that it is difficult to distinguish the date or characteristics of the coin.

Occasional hoards are discovered in the Philippines or in Mexico, but these are quickly absorbed by collectors, for the coin is very popular and since *Dos Mundos* was legal tender in the United States, it belongs in collections of U.S. Dollars.

The 4 *reale* or half-dollar size pieces are all scarce or rare. Eventually, this denomination was minted in smaller quantities, or most of the coins were cut into sections for use in the West Indies, where many of the Spanish coins were cut into sections or segments. It is from these sections, incidentally, that the terms, "two bits" and "four bits," still used today first originated.

The 2 reale, 1 reale, and ½ reale pieces are frequently encountered, but are not common in excellent condition.

Silver hoards discovered in many sections of the United States have been found to contain the Pillar pieces and it is not unusual to find them with any lot of old coins dated before 1860.

The *Pillar* 8 *reale* dollar will probably always be known as the world's most famous international Trade Dollar.

"No search upon the seas shall be"

One of the great moments in English Naval history was the capture of Porto Bello and Carthagena from the Spaniards in 1740.

During the early years of the eighteenth century, England's international prestige had declined so that Admiral Vernon's naval victory stirred a tremendous sense of patriotic pride and enthusiasm throughout Great Britain and the Colonies.

Admiral Edward Vernon was born in 1684 in Westminster, England. Trained from his early years for a career in the navy, at eighteen he was commissioned a second lieutenant. In 1706, he became the Commander of the frigate *Dolphin* and in 1707, was promoted to the command of the larger frigate *Jersey*, and sent on a tour of duty to the West Indies, where his duties included watching the Spanish fleet at Carthagena.

Later Edward Vernon was sent to the Baltic in command of the fifty-gun ship, the *Assistance,* and then of the *Grafton,* with seventy guns. In Britain's Parliament, Vernon served for a time as representative of the constituency of Ipswich. He criticized the government and the naval ministry and received considerable public acclaim for his forthright stand.

The fortified harbor of Porto Bello on the Isthmus of Panama had been one of Spain's most important colonial towns for more than two centuries. Spanish galleons filled with treasure from distant colonial points were brought there to be fitted out for the gruelling return voyage to Spain.

All of the nations with which Spain was at war cast envious eyes at Porto Bello from which Spanish gunboats prowled under the protective cover of the harbor fortifications. The Spaniards would stop all British ships that came their way, board them under pretext of searching for contraband goods, and claim the ships as prizes, treating the British sailors with abominable cruelty. (It was for exactly the same practices on the part of the British that the Americans fought the War of 1812).

In 1739, Vernon, then an Admiral of the British fleet, sailed for the West Indies with nine men-of-war. Leaving three ships in Jamaica, he sailed with the remaining six for Porto Bello where his triumphant victory over the Spanish made him a national hero and March 12, 1740, a famous date in British naval history.

A tremendous number of commemorative medals were struck to honor the victory of Admiral Vernon. They were worn by people of all classes and ages, and used as tokens and currency, for chips in gambling, even as teething rings and toys for children. Struck in a variety of sizes, metals and designs, these medals state such popular mottos of the day as, THE BRITISH GLORY REVIVED, and THE SPANISH PRIDE

Admiral Vernon Token

HUMBLED. There are approximately two hundred different pieces known and it is always possible for new varieties to come to light.

Medals were also issued for Carthagena and it is interesting to note that these were struck in honor of anticipated victories, for in spite of the fact that Vernon did have some success at Carthagena and landed forces on the Island of Cuba, illness and other serious difficulties made it necessary for him to return to Jamaica without actually capturing the city.

Slogans used on these commemorative medals included: BRAVE VERNON MADE US FREE / NO SEARCH UPON THE SEAS SHALL BE / ADMIRAL VERNON TOOK PORTO BELLO WITH SIX SHIPS ONLY.

Many of the reverses are engraved with minute details showing the various ships and Porto Bello tower and two steeples, buildings, etc.

Some of the medals bear the word, 'Havannah" and it is odd that the name of that city was used, since Vernon did not attack Havana. Possibly an attack on Havana was expected and the medals were struck in premature honor of the event.

Subsequently, Vernon did sail for Cuba, landing a small part of his group, making plans to reach Santiago and Havana. Persistent illness among the crew, however, finally made him return again to Jamaica.

The Germans struck medals commemorating the anticipated capture of Paris during World War I, and since this goal was never realized these medals became collectors' items. The same situation prevailed with the Admiral Vernon Havana Medals, when medals were struck in expectation of a great victory that never materialized.

Some of the Medals of Vernon with the Porto Bello reverse have six ships sailing to the right, six ships sailing to the left; others have five ships sailing to the right and one to the left; or four ships sailing to the right and two to the left; three ships sailing to the right and three to the left, etc.

These classifications give some indication of interesting possibilities in collecting this series, which is a joy to the variety collector.

There were many interesting satirical pieces issued because

of the unpopular ministry of Sir Walpole—one of which has the legend, MAKE ROOM FOR SIR ROBERT, and shows a devil leading Sir Robert Walpole by a rope around his neck into the open mouth of a dragon. Some of the pieces show full length figures of Admiral Vernon and Commodore Brown on the obverse. Brown was second in command and came in for his own share of plaudits from the excited and enthusiastic Englishmen.

An Admiral with the unusual name of Haddock was sent to the Mediterranean with the explicit job of preventing the union of the French and Spanish Fleets. It was believed that his instructions from the Admiralty forced him to curtail his efforts and the Admiral met with no success.

One unusual medal shows Admiral Haddock in his resplendent uniform, wearing a cocked hat. His hand is over the muzzle of a cannon, a ship is sailing on the right, and a fort appears on the left.

Collecting this series can again indicate the scope of knowledge and the sense of history that is a fascinating dividend in the realm of numismatics.

III

Putting Your Dollars into Coins; Numismatics for Investment and Speculation

It is estimated that in the United States there are five to ten million coin collectors of which the great majority are investors or speculators who have come into the numismatic field during the last few years.

The numismatist was formerly pictured poring over his coins and books in dim, hermit-like seclusion, studying the collection that he loved for its aesthetic beauty, and its evocations of history and art.

The new kind of collector or investor comes from every walk of life, is alert, aware of trends, often uses the teletype to keep up with the times, and is interested in coins mostly to make money.

The traditional collector is far from extinct, but the new breed of collector has given numismatics a modern approach and an air of business investment.

In the summer of 1965, the first minor recession in investment material took place and the coin investors who had previously bought from one party and sold to another, and always at a profit, began to realize that even in so stable an investment as coins, when prices become inflated, a levelling-off period is inevitable.

Economists and government officials have blamed the coin investors for the shortage of hard money, when for a period, in some parts of the country, change in various denominations actually had to be rationed. Even with the mints working seven days a week on round-the-clock schedules, the demand could not be met. What was not taken into consideration, however, was the growth in population, the tremendous number of coin-operated vending machines, and the closing of the San Francisco Mint a few years previously, all of which combined to cause the sudden shortage. There is no doubt that dealers, collectors, and investors hoarding sacks and rolls of coins did aggravate an already bad situation, but this was only one part of the problem.

Instead of the dingy, dusty stereotype of an old-fashioned coin shop, where the dealer often could not find the material his customers sought, the typical new coin shop or dealer's office may feature a teletype machine—nicknamed "The Monster"—of the kind found in stock brokerage offices. These teletypes tie together groups of dealers throughout the United States and Canada, enabling them to reach each other with information and requests at a moment's notice. Some dealers have boards on which the latest price quotations are posted.

Perpetual inventories are maintained, so that information on date, condition, roll, or sack is instantly available as well as the price. A few dealers have even installed salesmen who give advice and aid to investors, exactly like customers' men in stock brokerages. One enterprising Canadian firm has even sent men out selling coin investments from door to door.

Most of these coin investment houses have tie-ins with

finance companies or banks to help finance customers' purchases on the basis of weekly or monthly payments. Some companies are strictly numismatic investment-minded, while others handle collectors' material as well. Many maintain lavish offices, much like those of a fine stock brokerage.

U.S. War Nickel

One item that has been hoarded and eventually smelted is the *U.S. war nickel*. During World War II when all available nickel was needed for the defense program, the government changed the composition of the U.S. five cent piece from 75% copper - 25% nickel to 35% silver - 56% copper - 9% manganese. These were struck from October 11, 1942, to December 31, 1945. As a result of the constant rise in the price of silver, the silver content of each of these nickels is now worth more than seven cents, making the silver value greater than the face value of the coin itself.

Dealers have been purchasing these "war nickels" for some time and paying a premium over face value for them.

Until recently, there was no law that prohibited smelting silver coins or shipping them out of the country for that purpose. A new law now prohibits the smelting of U.S. silver coinage.

1950 Denver Mint Nickel

A highly publicized coin that has been consistently brought to the attention of the public is the 1950 *Denver Mint nickel* There were 2,630,000 minted, making this the smallest mintage of any Jefferson nickel. They brought small premiums when first released and have consistently improved in value, until in June of 1965 a roll of 40 reached a peak of over $1,000. While its value has since had its ups and downs, this still seems to be one of the most sought after coins, both to fill up sets of Jefferson nickels and for speculative investment against future rise.

One should be careful when buying this coin, as many of the pieces were poorly struck, and condition is very important since only coins in top condition will bring top prices.

More coins investors in the past put their money into rolls of 1960 to 1964 dates than any other series. It was generally considered that these were a good investment; they gained in value steadily, showing excellent returns and profits.

Recently the picture has changed because with the Mints turning out millions of coins in a steady stream, it is no longer advantageous to hoard the late date coins for there are more available than will ever be needed by any army of collectors. The investment basis on rolls from these large mintages has virtually disappeared. On the other hand, the investors who were fortunate enough to put away the older material of the "key" or scarce dates, found that their investment had weathered the storm, for there is always a demand for those coins with small mintages.

Except for the key or scarce dates, most of the rolls and sacks which were put away were brand new or uncirculated coins.

U.S. Proof Sets

The next most widely sought coin investments are the *U.S. Proof Sets*. This is a set of coins made at the U.S. Mint, especially struck for collectors, consisting of the 1¢, 5¢, 10¢, 25¢, and 50¢ pieces. These have sold at prices ranging from $1.89 to $2.10 in fairly recent years. Mintages were low until only a few years ago when there was a marked increase in the number struck each year. The 1964 sets, containing the Kennedy half-dollar, were oversubscribed immediately, and proved to be an excellent investment. While no sets were struck in 1965, they were again struck in 1968 at the U.S. Assay Office in San Francisco, California and for the first time are mintmarked "S" on each coin. Three million sets at $5.00

per set were sold.

Various investment and consumers' magazines, like the *Wall Street Journal, The Kiplinger Report,* and others, have carried stories on the investment phase of numismatics, mentioning the U.S. Proof Sets. These have attracted many non-collectors to the field.

Other investors purchase silver dollars, key coins, type coins, and other series because they feel these have the best potential.

One of the most important aspects of investing is training yourself, or dealing only with someone well qualified to give advice in this area. There are many reliable dealers specializing in investment who have had the necessary experience to give proper advice. But there are also those with "get rich quick" schemes who suggest that *everything* is a good investment. Those are the men to avoid.

Type Coin Collections

I recommend "type" coins for investment. A "type" coin is one coin selected from an entire series, such as an Indian Head Cent, a Lincoln cent, a 2¢ piece, a 3¢ piece (silver), a 3¢ piece (nickel), a shield type nickel, etc. The least expensive coin in this series and in the finest condition possible is used in making up a "type" set. In this way the rare and scarce dates are often avoided.

For many years the U.S. collector filled out a board by date and mintmark. This method brought millions of new collectors into the field, but each succeeding year saw prices of all the numismatic material increase, until the average collector could no longer afford to complete his sets. A series of coin boards and holders were then issued for only dates, leaving out the mintmarks, but even this method proved too costly, and the trend has veered to type coins.

As early as 1960, I saw a definite trend to type collecting and predicted this would be the popular numismatic medium

An early United States 1795 Half Dollar Second year of Issue. Coin does not have a denomination.

of the future. A type set is both interesting and informative for it shows the entire history of coinage of the United States. Some series, such as Lincoln cents, Jefferson nickels, Mercury dimes, and most modern coins require only one or two pieces for a Type set. It is when dealing with the earlier issues that collecting Type coins becomes more interesting and—sometimes—more involved.

As more and more of these coins go into permanent collections, they will be more difficult to obtain and will consequently enjoy a steady increase in value, making them fine potentials for investment, and will pay real dividends of pleasure in numismatics.

A collection of one of each of the U.S. commemorative type fifty cent pieces fits into this category and make a beautiful historical collection. An example of collecting types in the U.S. large cent would be as follows: 1793, Chain type; 1793, Wreath type; 1793, Strawberry Leaf; 1793-1796, Liberty cap; 1796-1807, Draped bust; 1808-1814, Turban head; 1816-1839, Coronet type; 1839-1857, Braided Hair.

There are also many interesting varieties and sub-varieties. The 1793 Chain, for example, comes with the word "Ameri" on one coin and "America" on another.

1801 United States Large Cent
The unusual three error variety may be seen on the reverse. Only one stem, 1/000, and two II instead of the letter "U" in "United."

The 1793 Wreath type has vine and bars on one edge; while another has a lettered edge, with one leaf; and still another, a lettered edge with a double leaf.

There are many varieties of 1794, 1795, and one 1796 has an error with the word Liberty being spelled "Liherty." Some large cents come with overdates, some with the gripped or milled edge, some with stems on the wreath, and some without.

One very unusual variety is the 1801 with three errors. One comes 1/000, 1 stem, and IINITED.

Other large cents come with large and small dates, broken dies, blunt I and pointed 1; some with twelve stars and some with thirteen stars; others with wide and close dates.

The 1839 large cents are unusual in themselves as you will see by their nicknames; Silly Head; The Booby Head; The Type of 1838; The Type of 1840; The Overdate, 1839 over '36. The 1855 coin comes with slanting 5's and also with a knob on the Liberty Head's ear.

The U.S. half-dollars make a wonderful type set. The 1796 comes with fifteen stars and with sixteen stars. Both types are rare. The 1803 comes with a small 3 and with a large 3; the 1805, '06, and other dates have overdates.

One interesting example is the 1806 half-dollar. This comes overdated 1806 over 1805; then there is an 1806 over an inverted 6. There is also a round top 6 with large stars, a round top 6 with small stars, a pointed top 6 with a stem through claw, and a pointed top 6 without stem through claw. The possibilities for research and compilation can be illustrated by this one date alone.

The 1807 comes with a bust facing right and also a bust facing left. The 1811 comes with a period between the 18 and the 11.

The other dates of half-dollars have many unusual varieties, but an interesting one is the 1823 which comes with the broken 3, patched 3 and ugly 3.

Some collectors like to have one of each mintmark in their type collections to show the various Mints which issued coins for the particular series.

There are hundreds of other varieties, but this should suggest the unlimited possibilities in only one series, outside of the collecting by date.

The U.S. Colonial series, from the Pine Tree Shilling to the Washington pieces, bring to mind the Pilgrims and the Revolutionary War, and the striking of the first official U.S. coins in 1793. The colonial series covers most of the original thirteen Colonies and is of interest both to the collector and non-collector.

Few people collect gold pieces by date and mintmark since the cost would be prohibitive to the average collector. Accordingly, most gold collectors are type collectors.

The most popular series, next to the U.S., are the Canadian coins, both for collecting and investing.

1797 United States Large Cent (obverse) Struck a little off center, this coin is popular with collectors of error coins.

1803 United States Large Cent
Mint error at upper left shows two figures of another date.

The collector of Canadian coins now faces the same situation that existed in the U.S. recently. The completion of the regular series is becoming too costly for the average collector and many have turned to type collecting. As the popularity of type collecting increases more numismatic supplies and albums will be issued to help the collector with his sets.

One way to start a type set is to take a Canadian 1965 proof-like set consisting of the 1¢, 5¢, 10¢, 25¢, 50¢ and $1 pieces and use the individual coins, which of course are in the finest possible condition. These coins bear the likeness of Queen Elizabeth II, representing her as the more mature Queen. A 1964 proof-like set could also be broken up to show a different type, including the commemorative dollar.

1797 United States Silver Dollar

1965 Canadian Five Cent Piece

It is essential to obtain coins in the finest possible condition except in a series where pieces are rather expensive and seldom obtainable. Then one might settle for coins in (very) fine or (extra) fine condition. Eventually, it might be necessary to seek out coins in lower grades, as those in better condition become more difficult to obtain, so the time to begin a Canadian type set is NOW!

Canadian type coins can be expected to mount steadily in value and in some cases, shortages will undoubtedly develop.

Of special interest are coins like the 1858 *twenty cent piece,* since this denomination was issued only once. Many of these have been melted down and used for jewelry over the years.

Canadian silver dollars of the years 1935, '39, '49, '58, and '64 have already become quite popular and as the popularity of type collecting increases these coins will continue to appeal to both collectors and investors alike.

In the Victoria type coins, uncirculated coins are becoming more and more difficult to obtain and collectors may have to settle for a "Very Fine" or "Extra Fine" condition coin if they cannot afford to purchase these coins in top condition.

The coins of Edward VII will improve in value in years to come since large numbers of these are being put into type sets. Fairly low mintages and a tendency of the coins to wear quickly, contribute to the difficulty of obtaining these items in top condition.

The various series from 1¢, 5¢, 10¢, 25¢, 50¢, and silver dollar of the three rulers, George V, 1922-36; George VI, 1937-52; and Queen Elizabeth, 1953-, are usually stocked by most dealers in all conditions and there should be no question about obtaining these in condition desired.

Many new collectors are amazed to find that Canada has issued twenty cent pieces and small five cent silver coins. These obsolete coins always attract a great deal of attention when shown to the novice collector.

1955 Lincoln Cent (double die)

It is hoped that when the supply manufacturers create the new holders and boards for collecting type sets, they will eliminate many of the minor coin varieties that are not needed. For instance, in collecting U.S. coins, the 1955 *Double Die cent*—obtainable for a very nominal sum until it was listed in the Guide Book and placed in the coin board—skyrocketed in value from a few dollars to several hundred.

Many advanced collectors make up their own holders or obtain holders with blank spaces allowing them to place such items as re-engraved dates, small and large dates, small leaves and broad leaves, dot coins, and other varieties. This procedure enables them to go as far as they wish in adding styles or varieties to meet their personal interests.

One field that should not be overlooked is collecting coins of the Canadian Provinces. Only one coin was issued for Prince Edward Island, the 1¢ piece of 1871. Four hundred thousand were coined and while this coin is very easily obtained in ordinary condition, it is scarce and rare in top conditions and "Brilliant Uncirculated" coins bring a high price. This coin is also going into foreign type coin collections, inasmuch as it is the only coin for Prince Edward Island.

New Brunswick issued both large cents and half cents. The *half cent* is a very scarce item and difficult to obtain in top condition. Since only a small number of these pieces are available, this should be one of the first pieces to skyrocket when collectors turn to this series.

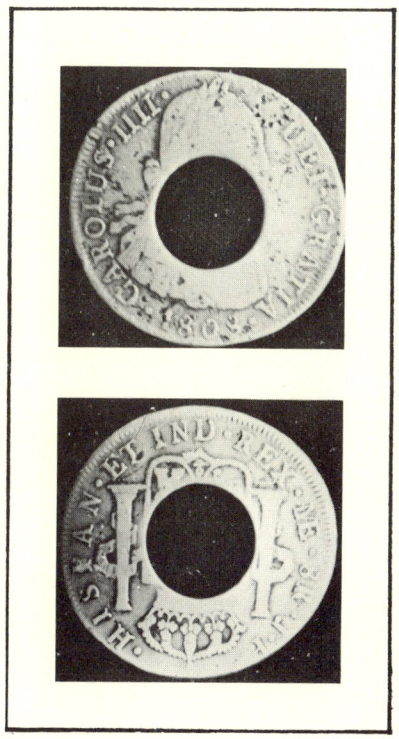

Prince Edward Island *Holey* Dollar (beware of forgeries)

Although there is a tendency for the better grade coins to increase in price, the New Brunswick *large cents* dated 1861 and 1864 are easily obtained, except in "Uncirculated" or "Full Red" condition.

None of the silver New Brunswick coins of the 5¢, 10¢, and 20¢ denominations are common. Mintages are low, and many of these coins are seen in poor and mutilated condition. Coins of this type should be obtained in the best condition possible for their value will be considerably enhanced over the years.

Nova Scotia has two type coins. The 1¢ of 1861 and 1864 are easily obtainable, while the scarce 1862 date can be by-passed for a type set. Again, these coins, easily obtainable in ordinary condition, are becoming more and more difficult to obtain in the top grades.

The Nova Scotia half-cents of 1861 and 1864 are, in my opinion, the "sleepers" of the Canadian Provincial series. They remain inexpensive, but will be absorbed by both Canadian and foreign collectors and are currently the least expensive of the obsolete half-cents.

Newfoundland One Cent, 1929
1947 was the last year Newfoundland coins were issued.

The coins of Newfoundland have been highly touted for many years and it is only a matter of time until they come into their own. Mintages are extremely low and many coins have been melted and destroyed. A small new group of type collectors throughout the world could easily liquidate the Newfoundland coin stocks now in dealers' hands.

Observe the size of a few of the Newfoundland coin mintages:

Large Cents:	1885 —	40,000
	1888 —	50,000
Five Cent:	1876 —	20,000
	1885 —	16,000
	1946 —	2,041
Ten Cent:	1876 —	10,000
	1880 —	10,000
	1885 —	8,000
Twenty Cent:	1873 —	45,000
	1880 —	30,000
Fifty Cent:	1880 —	24,000
	1888 —	20,000
	1894 —	40,000

Even the $2 gold piece issued in 1872 were only 6,000, while in 1880 only 2,500 of the $2 gold piece were minted.

It is interesting to compare these extremely low mintages with the standards established by other countries.

With Newfoundland coins very difficult to obtain in nice condition—especially the Edward VII and Victoria series—it is easy to understand how a type set of these pieces will prove beneficial to investment holdings in the numismatic field.

The Proof-like sets of Canada, called "Mint Sets" by the Canadian Government, are issued each year. Many investors have realized appreciable profits in this particular series although at present, they are in the doldrums. In 1954, only 7,400 sets were issued and as recently as 1960, only 64,000 were issued. Since then, quantities have doubled and tripled until the number of sets issued now is in the millions. Because of the low mintages, the early sets will always be in demand and will be difficult to obtain. There are earlier Specimen or Proof Sets issued in the years 1858, 1870, 1902, 1908, 1911, and 1937. Prices of these vary from several hundred dollars to several thousand and because of their scarcity, these sets are not frequently offered.

For both fascinating historical lore and for sound investment, nothing can surpass type set collecting.

Foreign Proof Sets

A relatively new investment medium is collecting *Foreign Proof Sets*. Most of these sets were issued in small and limited quantities for coin collectors in the various countries, and the demand for them is constantly rising. The Philippines, for instance, issued Proof Sets from 1903 to 1908, in quantities of only 500 to 1,000 sets. These Proofs are eagerly sought by collectors, many of whom keep them along with their U.S. collections. Again, because of the small number minted, Australia and South Africa Proof Sets—including those of recent issue—bring excellent prices and are in considerable demand.

The New Zealand Proof Set of 1935 containing the rare Waitangi Crown issued in comemoration of the silver jubilee of King George V brings more than $1500.

The 1911 and the 1937 British Proof Sets with gold sell at close to a thousand dollars per set, as do the Southern Rhodesia Sets of 1932 and 1937.

Many of the new nations of Africa, Malawi and Zambia, for example, are issuing Proof Sets that are being released

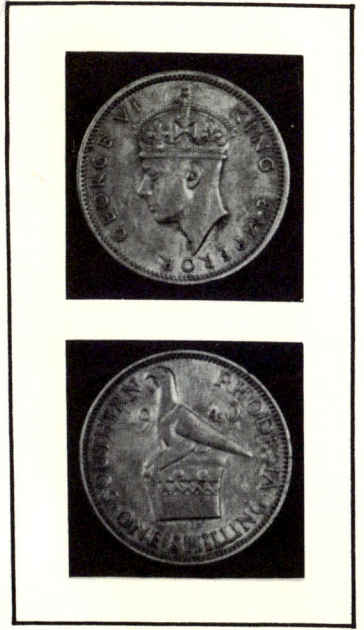

Southern Rhodesian One Shilling Silver Coin
Coins of this new country have become very popular

through three London coin dealers on a "one to a customer" basis.

Proof Sets can be expected to have a great future, since every one of these items was made especially for collectors.

Gold coins have always been hoarded and in some Far Eastern countries women hoard their family fortunes in gold jewelry, worn right on their person. Much gold has been hoarded on the assumption that the $35-per-ounce price will be increased and that gold coins, common or otherwise, will increase accordingly in value. U.S. $20 gold pieces are an exception for they have not gone up in price since 1945 when they were valued at $85 and today's market price is lower at $60-$70. At the time of World War II, gold coins were in great demand, and the prices reached then have never been equalled.

The French, because of their frequently fluctuating economy, have not trusted their own currency and always considered gold to be the world's most stable investment. Today the French remain among the world's greatest gold hoarders.

Some countries have struck coins especially for the convenience of bullion purchasers and investors. In Venezuela, the Banco-Italo-Venezolano, struck a very unusual *General MacArthur* coin, that is not very well known—a 222 gram gold piece with a reeded edge.

These pieces, struck in four sizes and issued as part of the "Chiefs of the Second War" 1939-45 series, have a handsome bust of the General. Because U.S. laws prohibit the importation of most gold coins, very few have entered this country.

With so much activity in coin speculation and investment, it was natural that corporations interested in wholesale and retail coin business would be formed and that there would be an increase in the "brokerage" aspect of the coin business.

Even the Federal Securities Exchange Commission has become interested in the numismatic field and looked into some of the brokerage-type activities conducted by certain coin dealers without experience, without licenses, where customers' accounts, in some cases, were not segregated but included with the firm's own. Investigations and checks were made in a number of cases. There is a possibility that eventually the SEC might want to control certain aspects of the coin investment field.

Recently, a number of books and pamphlets have appeared as guides to the investor. These have charts showing increases over the years and projecting future values on the basis of past performance. I think that charts in the numismatic field are a poor means of planning or projecting investments. It will take a recession and a depression in coins to make enough information available for these charts to be as widely used as stock charts are in the stock brokerage firms.

Most investors have placed their holdings in modern coins. To them, I would suggest, as a hedge, the purchasing of earlier type coins, key coins, and other stable numismatic material, which is only offered at times as individual pieces or in small quantities. These pieces were not minted in large numbers. Many have been destroyed or damaged over the years. These items have enjoyed a steady upswing for many years. These pieces are even desirable at present since there is a collectors' market for them. Coin rolls and bags, on the other hand, are usually investment material with which one must wait for the growth of a market through an increased number of collectors. Collectors with only five or ten years experience can attest to the remarkable increase in demand and value of the older coins and keys. Even collectors who purchased one of each for their collections are amazed when faced with the prices being asked for this material today.

Some schools and universities have numismatic courses with a marked accent on investments but anyone seriously interested in coin investment should really take a thorough course in coin collecting. This would cover such topics as

Building a Library
Joining a Coin Club
Grading Coins
Cleaning and Repairing Coins
What to Collect
Token Collecting
Paper Money Collecting
Supplies and Aids to the Investor and Collector
Classification of Coins

Numismatic Economics
Foreign Proof Sets
Foreign Coin Collecting
Early U.S. Coins.

These topics represent only part of the curriculum which I gave at the Massachusetts Institute of Technology where there was one session devoted to investments only. Many students are originally drawn to these classes by the profit motive, but later find that by absorbing the various phases of the subject, they become knowledgeable and well informed in a short period of time. Then rather than groping in the dark, they have answers to many questions a less broadly based course could not encompass.

Since 1955, there has been a rise in the stock market, in the value of antiques, of paintings, and of other collector items. Coins have far outdistanced all other collection items with a tremendous percentage rise.

Many astute companies have placed coin investments in their portfolios and some insurance companies, having obtained permission from the Insurance Commissioners, now include Proof Sets and other material in their holdings Groups of professional people, including a large group on the West Coast, labor unions, industrial firms, and other organizations with funds to invest have their statisticians and investment counsellors scanning the market for sound coin purchases.

Any responsible broker's advice is: Do not gamble unless you can afford to lose! There are periods when coin values go down and the investor must be in a position to wait until the market is ready to support a further rise in prices. Sometimes this may entail waiting for an extended period. There is no substitute for a knowledgeable and reliable consultant to advise the investor, and this advice is especially important to the novice.

Clubs and Organizations

Why not join a coin club or numismatic organization where you will meet a friendly and stimulating group of people, both beginners and advanced collectors? There are always old-timers with specialized knowledge, and lectures are frequently given. There are thousands of clubs throughout the U.S. and Canada where new members are warmly received.

There are also many regional and national organizations like the American Numismatic Association, which publishes its own excellent monthly magazine called *The Numismatist*.

The American Numismatic Society is the oldest and most respected organization in the country. It maintains a museum in New York City where students from all over the world come to study.

The Canadian Numismatic Association, the second largest coin collectors group, has grown very rapidly in recent years because of the renewed interest in Canadian numismatics.

Among nationally and internationally recognized organizations of coin dealers are the International Association of Professional Numismatists, Professional Numismatists Guild, Retail Coin Dealers' Association, and Professional Numismatic Guild of Canada. These groups are regulated by rules which benefit both the buyer and the seller who guarantees satisfaction.

* *

To sum up my findings in this investment field, there will be setbacks and drops in the coin market when overspeculation is prevalent, but just as the stock market has revived many times from its setbacks, so will the coins continue to move forward over the years, and at a more accelerated pace. In over fifty years in numismatics, I have found that collectors and dealers have constantly complained about high and inflated prices and yet each year, with very few exceptions, prices have continued to rise steadily.

IV

■

A Guide for the New Numismatist
Fundamentals of a Coin Collection

The simplest beginning of a coin collection in the United States is to look through your daily change and retain the dates and mintmarks needed to fill the empty spaces in a coin holder.

These holders are available for coins from the 1¢ denomination to $1.00. There are special folders for type collectors that are made blank so that any suitable collection could be put together with individual labeling. Depending on the type and construction, the price of these coin boards ranges from 35¢ to several dollars each.

Millions of the 35¢ boards are sold annually to beginners, and while these boards are not recommended for the advanced collector, they do serve the purpose and have the spaces necessary to place the coins with the proper date and mintmark designated. The manufacturers are constantly improving the quality of such supplies and are now manufacturing coin holders for many other countries, but particularly for Canada, Mexico, Great Britain, and Australia.

Many collectors start with the 1¢ pieces and work their way up to the higher denomination. The time comes when the pieces needed for the collection are more and more difficult to obtain. At that point some collectors trade or sell their duplicates in order to obtain funds with which to purchase needed items. That stage is when the collector finds that it is difficult to get along without a coin dealer.

The coin dealer stocks coins not found in circulation. It is important to make contact with a reliable and reputable dealer.

Roosevelt Dime

Dates and mintmarks are easily obtainable. Issued from 1946 to date, they are very popular with collectors.

His experience and knowledge will make doing business with such a dealer extremely valuable to a collector lacking the knowledge and ready information of the professional. If a dealer does not have needed information available, he knows how to obtain it.

Some of the most famous numismatists have been coin dealers. They have contributed to the field of numismatics through writings, research, and lectures; the trend toward education in numismatics has been encouraged chiefly by the dealers throughout Canada and the United States who are promoting and guiding this most important phase of coin collecting.

One method of determining a dealer's rating would be through the organizations with which he is affiliated. The Professional Numismatist Guild, The International Association of Professional Numismatists, Retail Coin Dealers' Association, and Professional Numismatic Guild of Canada require certain standards of dealers who join their ranks and complaints to these organizations receive prompt attention.

GLOSSARY

BILLON: An alloy of gold or silver with a large amount of baser metal such as copper.

COMMEMORATIVE COIN: Issued to honor an individual, an event or an anniversary.

COUNTERSTAMPS: Advertising, names, initials, words slogans, or symbols that have been stamped on a coin after striking.

FIELD: The blank space forming a background for the design.

FILLER: A poor coin which is only used to fill in a set until a better specimen can be obtained.

FREAKS: Coins oddly struck, with the result that they may be off center, bear a double date, struck from a thin planchet, etc.

INSCRIPTION: The numbers and lettering on a coin.

INCUSE: Design stamped in rather than raised.

LEGEND: The inscription on a coin.

LETTERED EDGE: Lettering around the edge of the coin, used for a number of years, usually before 1837.

MILLED EDGE: Even ridges on the edge of the coin is called "Milling."

MINTMARK: The letter on the coin to indicate where the coin was minted.

MULE: A coin produced by using the obverse die of one coin and the reverse die of another.

OBVERSE: The face or front of the coin.

OFF CENTER: A coin struck out of alignment, caused by the planchet moving in the process of striking.

OVERDATE: Changing a date at the mint, sometimes due to the shortage of dies. It is sometimes difficult for the engraver to cover the previous date completely.

PATTERNS: Pieces which are minted and submitted as a design for new coinage. They are struck in limited number and are usually found in various metals.

PLANCHET: The blanks or pieces of metal used in striking coins.

REVERSE: The back of the coin.

TOKEN: A coin not backed by the government, but circulated and accepted as money. Many pieces were used for advertising, trading, etc., and were struck by private individuals or companies.

UNIQUE: A coin or piece of which only one specimen is known.

VARIETY: Coins of the same date and denomination on which the mintmark may be large or small, the date slanted differently, or with any one of hundreds of minor variations.

MINTMARKS

INDIAN CENTS: Only issued with mintmarks two years, 1908 and 1909. If San Francisco Mint, has an S under the wreath on the reverse side.

LINCOLN CENT: Mintmark appears under the date.

3¢ SILVER: Only the 1851, New Orleans Mint, comes with a letter "o" mintmark which is found on the reverse side.

LIBERTY NICKEL: Only one date, the 1912, comes with a mintmark. The S for San Francisco and the D for Denver are found on the reverse to the left of the word "Cents."

BUFFALO NICKEL: The mintmark is on the reverse, under the words "five Cents" and will be either S or D.

JEFFERSON NICKEL: The mintmark is on the reverse, at the right of the building. The silver pieces issued from 1942 to 1945 have the mintmark above the dome.

HALF-DIME: The reverse will have the O or S mintmark, either below or above the wreath.

DIME (Liberty Seated): Below or above the wreath, on reverse.

MERCURY DIME: Will show the mintmark to the left of the fasces.

ROOSEVELT DIME: The mintmark appears at the left bottom of torch. All of the mintmarks of the dimes 1916 to date appear on the reverse.

TWENTY CENT PIECE: Mintmark on reverse under the eagle.

QUARTER DOLLAR (Liberty Seated type): Mintmark appears on reverse under eagle.

QUARTER DOLLAR (Standing Liberty): Beginning with 1916, mintmark is on the obverse or front of coin, to the left of date.

QUARTER DOLLAR (Washintgon): First minted in 1932. The mintmark appears on the reverse, under the eagle.

HALF DOLLAR (Liberty Seated type, Liberty Head type): Mintmark appears on reverse under the eagle. During 1916, the mintmark was shifted to the front of the coin. In 1917, it appears two ways: on the obverse and on the reverse. On the dates after 1917, the mintmark appears on the lower left reverse.

HALF DOLLAR (Franklin or Liberty Bell type which first appeared in 1948): Mintmark under the word "States."

HALF DOLLAR (Liberty Seated): Mintmark appears on the reverse, under the eagle.

DOLLAR (Peace type first coined in 1921): Mintmark under the eagle's feathers, on the reverse.

DOLLAR (Trade type): Mintmark appears on the reverse under the eagle.

$2.50 GOLD PIECE (dates from 1840 to 1907): Mintmarks appear on the reverse, under the eagle.

THE INDIAN TYPE GOLD (issued from 1908 to 1929): The mintmark is on the lower left reverse of the coin.

$5.00 GOLD: Mintmarks follow the same pattern as on the $2.50 gold.

$3.00 GOLD: Mintmarks under the wreath on the reverse.

$10.00 GOLD: Mintmarks appear on the reverse, under the eagle, except on those issued after 1907, on which they appear at the left of value.

$20.00 GOLD (Dates before 1907): The mintmark appears on the reverse, under the eagle.

$20.00 GOLD (more recent dates): Mintmark on the obverse under the date.

Coin Library

Both neophyte and advanced collector should have a numismatic library. If you start with one good book and add to it gradually, you will find them invaluable when you need reference information or when purchasing coins for your collection.

Very few coin publications were available a number of years ago, but today new ones come out each month. A good coin dealer can give advice on books that will be especially helpful with a collection. Thousands of books are covered in the excellent bibliography compiled by Mrs. V. Clain-Stefanelli, who is affiliated with the Numismatic section of the Smithsonian Institute in Washington, D. C. Nearly all public libraries now have books on coin collecting and some even have the weekly coin papers and trade magazines available. A small personal library will be invaluable and will pay the original investment many times over in knowledge, information, and convenience.

I also recommend subscribing to one or more coin newspapers or magazines. *Coin World* is a weekly paper that has a great deal of coin information in addition to its advertisements and trading post.

Numismatic News follows a similar style, and is a weekly. It is a well recognized publication in its field.

Numismatic Scrapbook, a magzine of many years standing, is an established monthly. It can be very helpful.

Others, including *Coins and Coinage,* are available by single issue at newstands and drugstores, as well as by subscription.

World Coins is the first monthly publication catering exclusively to the foreign coin collector.

There are many others to choose from, depending on individual interests. I do not recommend subscribing to every coin magazine and paper, but there are certain publications that will be of help to each particular phase of collecting.

Many coin dealers issue price lists that are obtainable free or for a postage stamp. Some of these lists are invaluable for checking up-to-date prices and forecasting trends.

As a rule, once a customer makes a purchase, dealers will place his name on their mailing list, and will continue to send him timely information.

Grading of Coins

In another chapter, we will list the various conditions which are used in grading coins. This is of utmost importance, whether one is buying or selling.

After a hundred years of American numismatics, a book has finally been published by Whitman Publishing Company, authored by Brown and Dunn, which is now being accepted as a standard reference in the field of grading. Two of the top Canadian dealers have written grading catalogs that have become a "must" for collectors.

All of the standard catalogs and even the commercial publications detail in words and diagrams how to properly grade coins. This is still an intricate and difficult area but progress continues to be made.

How to Buy and Sell by Mail

Many millions of dollars are changing hands yearly in mail order coin transactions.

To purchase coins by mail from a dealer, check his advertisements. He will usually state the organizations he belongs to, how long he has advertised in the publication, and anything which might show prospective customers his reliability. This is a method of checking *his* references, the same as he would check yours.

All reliable dealers guarantee satisfaction on any merchandise purchased from them, provided coins are returned within a reasonable time—usually from three to ten days after receipt. The great majority of transactions are satisfactory in every way to both seller and buyer. Occasionally, if there is any dissatisfaction, the return of the material and a refund check will straighten out the matter promptly. In the unusual case, a problem that is difficult to straighten out may arise. In this case the publisher of the magazine in which the dealer's ad appeared will usually stand behind the buyer and help him in any way possible, provided his demands are reasonable.

When ordering coins by mail, be sure to write legibly, have your name and return address on both envelope and order, and allow a reasonable length of time for completion of the transaction.

If you have credit references with any bank, department store, or coin company, it is very simple to receive coins on approval, and if prompt returns are made, future approvals become a matter of form.

When selling coins by mail, you will notice that dealers offer varying prices for the same condition coins. Reliability is just as important in doing business as the offer of a few cents more for an item.

When you ship your coins to a dealer, be sure to make up an inventory in duplicate, one which you will send with your package and one for your own records. Make certain that the material is well packaged and properly insured.

Many dealers will make you an offer and hold the coins, pending your acceptance or refusal. Should you refuse his offer, your coins are returned to you.

Disposing of Coins or Coin Collections

There are four major ways to dispose of an entire collection or of duplicate coins.

AUCTIONS: Coins are sold at a public or mail auction or both. A commission is charged by the dealer, depending on the type of material and auction held.

TELETYPE: This is the best medium for investment-type material, such as gold and proof sets. There is usually a close "buy and sell" market, to help the seller obtain the best possible price. Commissions charged by teletype dealers are usually reasonable because of the large volume of business they are able to handle.

CONSIGNMENT: This method takes longer to dispose of your material, but usually obtains the highest prices since dealers will list or offer coins at the market prices. They charge a commission—usually ten to twenty-five percent, depending on the material. Because the dealer does not have to invest in the material, he can afford to work on a smaller margin of profit.

OUTRIGHT CASH SALE: This is the method for the quickest disposal of coins or of a collection. Several dealers may be tried so that the highest price may be obtained, but in this method the seller is expected to accept a lower price for his numismatic material.

Handling and Cleaning Coins

Collections of coins should be properly stored in safes, cabinets, coin holders, etc. It is necessary to give your coins all the protection possible because if coins are not stored properly, they can turn color or carbon spots may form, and the value of the coin will be greatly diminished.

Unless coins are kept in a well constructed coin holder, they should be properly protected and wrapped. Many collectors use 2" x 2" envelopes, which fit most coin sizes. Better protection can be afforded by placing the coin in a cellophane envelope or similar covering before inserting it into the paper envelope. Information about the coin can be itemized on the front of the envelope, itemizing the type of coin, its condition, the price paid for it, etc. This may prove of great convenience to you later on.

There are coin albums on the market ranging in price from thirty-five cents to several dollars each. Plastic holders are frequently used for better coins, but these are much more expensive than ordinary coin holders.

There are various kinds of plastic tubes on the market for

the storage and safekeeping of rolls from cents to silver dollars. While these are fairly inexpensive, my own experience has been that a covering of aluminum foil gives a roll of coins excellent protection and has proved one of the best safeguards available.

Cleaning Coins

Do not undertake to clean a coin unless it is absolutely necessary and then do so only with expert advice. Be extremely careful. Indiscriminate cleaning can easily detract from the value of a coin or even ruin it.

Years ago, a famous household cleaning product was the most popular coin cleaner. People would often rub a little of this cleanser powder on their coins before taking them to offer to dealers. I have seen many rare coins diminish substantially in value because of having been cleaned in this manner. Dealers even began adopting the trade name of this cleanser as a watchword among themselves.

There are many new products for cleaning coins and it is best to contact your own coin dealer who will be glad to recommend the cleaners he has found to be most effective. He will also advise which products to stay away from.

Silver coins are the easiest to clean. For many years baking soda and water has been used for this purpose. Make a paste of the soda and water and rub the coin—including the edges—carefully. It will come out with a shiny new color, if it was uncirculated in the first place. This cleaning method will remove all the dirt and accumulation of the years.

Copper coins are a little more difficult to clean. A drop of sweet oil applied with a piece of flannel or other soft cloth, will remove dirt and film from the coin's surface.

The old-time collector liked his coins to keep the original patina. He felt that it had taken many years to produce the blue, golden, and other tones, which he regarded as the ultimate in perfection. This is where the phrase "toned uncirculated" originates.

One Method Not Recommended for Cleaning Coins

The late John LeBlanc, for many years one of Boston's best known coin dealers and numismatists, taught me a great deal about the wonderful hobby of numismatics. Whatever time I could spare, I would spend with him. Well known for his absent-mindedness, John was constantly making notations for himself. Hundreds of these self-reminders always garnished his desk.

One day he showed me a 1799 large cent—the rarest date and king of its series—he was preparing to clean. Some foreign material that could not be removed by ordinary methods had adhered to it over the years, so John told me he was going to give the coin a quick dip in nitric acid to see if this could be loosened or dissolved.

While I was engrossed in a small collection of coins lying on the desk, John put the coin into the prepared nitric acid solution. Just then, the telephone rang. I continued to examine the coins while John carried on his telephone conversation.

After quite a bit of discussion, John finally hung up. Suddenly he sprang into action again when he realized that he had left the coin in the nitric acid. A heavy silence prevaded the office when the 1799 Large Cent came into view. All that remained of the former rarity was a muddy-colored liquid, and the shell of a coin.

This was a real calamity, particularly in those depression days when any coin valued at several dollars or more represented a considerable sum of money. I have heard of other incidents along this line, so I advise extreme caution in handling acids or any strong caustic solutions in cleaning coins.

Counterfeits

There are many clever counterfeits, electrotypes, and cast copies of some of the rare early coins. When purchasing a rare or valuable coin, one should obtain a guarantee that it is genuine because the counterfeit pieces, especially those made in the 1880's, can easily trick the novice.

Most of the recent counterfeits feel greasy and have a dull sound. If counterfeits are lead or of some other poor composition, it is possible to cut the edge very easily. On a genuine coin, this is a very difficult task. On the genuine coins, the reeding will be even and distinct, while on many of the counterfeits, the edges are quite crude.

There are many appraisers and dealers who are specialists and can give a written guarantee for a small fee on the genuineness of any numismatic item.

In recent years, the tendency has been to alter dates and mintmarks, such as the scarce 1909-s vdb and 1914-d Lincoln cents. As the value has increased, more fakes have appeared on the market, making it quite important to know both the coins to be purchased and the dealer from whom they are being bought.

Fidos

There is a great deal of interest in the collecting of Mint Errors, Oddities, Freaks, and Variations. "Fido" is the word commonly applied to these.

For many years the traditional collector or dealer turned up his nose at all such oddities or minor variations. Everyone who concentrated on this kind of material was considered a "junk" collector.

In recent years, more and more articles and stories about this kind of oddity are noticed, along with "Letters to the Editors"

1964 error Lincoln Cent
This controversial coin has multiple strikings

pertaining to them. These coins are becoming more acceptable to both old and new collectors and their popularity will undoubtedly increase over the years.

Among this series are such interesting misspelling on Lincoln cents as AMESICA, LIBER7Y, 7TATES, LIBEXTY, LIBGRTY and LISERTY.

One of the finest aspects of collecting this kind of material is that new items can be found that have never before been listed, which is always a thrill to any collector.

There are many types of errors collected, including off-metal, off-center, multiple struck, oversized, thick, thin, rotated dies, blank planchets (these are the original pieces of metal used in the minting the coins) and a good many others.

In paper money, collectors search for seals inverted, seal on reverse, seal omitted, seal incomplete, irregular corners, double denomination, inverted reverse, signatures omitted, and various others.

Several collector groups have been formed for this specialized field and they are growing rapidly.

V

Hawaiian Script, Alaskan Bingles, and Puerto Rican Clay Faces

Numismatics of Hawaii

Hawaiian coins have always been of great interest to collectors, but since the Islands were admitted to statehood, a tremendous surge of enthusiasm has taken place in every phase of Hawaiian numismatics, including coins, tokens, and paper money.

After the arrival of Captain Cook in 1778, the Hawaiians used a variety of articles as money—nails, beads, bits of iron. Necessary trading was done by barter. During the 19th century, sandalwood became a medium of exchange between the Island chiefs and foreign traders until, with the reign of Kamehameha I, gold and silver were accepted as a medium of exchange.

Because of the scarcity of small foreign coins on the

Island, various individuals, firms, and institutions were given permission to make their own scrip.

The first token currency was issued at the Koloa Plantation in Kauai in 1836. The manager could not obtain enough coin to pay his men and issued scrip in 12-1/2¢, 25¢ and 50¢ denominations, which were redeemable at the plantation store. One unusual facet of this issue is that the scrip was overprinted on French theatre tickets. The values were of different sizes and were printed in Honolulu for the manager, William Hooper, who thought it would be very difficult to counterfeit money made with such an unusual background.

Other paper money was issued at the Mt. Pleasant Silk Plantation in Kauai during 1843 and 1844. In 1844 notes were also issued for the Wailuku Female Seminary when they were used for transactions between the school and students. These were printed by the Reverend Lorrin Andrews. Of extreme rarity in these are the Lahainaluna issue, in the following denominations: Hookahi Dala, or $1, Hapalua or $1/2, Hapaha or $1/4, Hapawalu or $1/8, Hapaumi or $1/16, 3 Keneta or 3¢. Some of the high school pupils assisted in engraving the copper plates that were used.

In 1883, Hawaii issued its first National Treasury Bills, now rare. A $1 bill dated 1893 has been discovered. It is crudely printed, "Hawaiian Island Provisional Government Will Pay," etc. Very little is known about this rarity.

During 1895, the American Banknote Company printed three series of Bills, including silver and gold certificates, all of which are very rare today. Later, U. S. notes on the Hawaiian Islands were treasury issues of gold certificates from $10 to 10,000, silver $1 certificates, U. S. $2 and $5 notes, National Bank notes from $5 to $100, and Federal Reserve notes from $5 to 10,000.

The small size notes with the Hawaiian overprint used during World War II are well known to collectors. These were issued in 1934 and 1935, in denominations of $1, $5, $10, and $20.

The $20 note of 1934 is quite scarce, but all of the other pieces are available.

Hard Money of the Islands

Very few coins were issued for the Kingdom of Hawaii. The first was a copper one cent piece bearing the head of Kamehameha III issued in 1847. The cents are all dated 1847 and are quite scarce and will be dealt with a little further in this chapter.

Hawaiian Dollar, 1883
Struck at the San Francisco Mint

The most famous issue of regular coinage is the series of 1883. These were issued in denominations of 10¢ or one dime, $1/4, $1/2, and $1. These were coined at the San Francisco Mint.

Five hundred thousand pieces of the $1/4 and $1 were struck, 700,000 of the half-dollar, and 250,000 of the dimes.

The great majority of the dollars were withdrawn from circulation and melted, leaving approximately ten percent of the issue outstanding. Many of these beautiful pieces found their way into various forms of jewelry. Many were drilled for use in bracelets and pendants.

All of the pieces except the $1/4 are very difficult to obtain in new condition. A small hoard of $1/4 in excellent condition did come to light a number of years ago.

The designs for these coins were prepared by the famous Charles Barber, Chief Engraver of the Philadelphia Mint, who engraved many American coins.

The Hawaiian Sesqui-centennial half-dollar was issued in 1928 with a striking of 10,008 pieces. This is one of the Commemorative half-dollars, with a catalog value of $650 in brand- new condition.

Fifty pieces, struck for presentation in Proof condition, catalog at $2,000 each. They originally were released to the public and collectors at $2.00 each in uncirculated condition. The presentation pieces were given to dignitaries and celebrities.

Medals

The English explorer, Captain James Cook, the first European to visit the Island, named the group The Sandwich Islands in honor of the Earl of Sandwich.

At the time of his landing in 1778, the Island was ruled by four native monarchs, each of whom ruled one area of the Island.

There were a number of orders issued by the Hawaiian kings which are quite rare. Four different orders were founded by King Kalakaua I to be presented to those who had made a noteworthy contribution to the king or government.

A number of medals were struck in 1959 to commemorate statehood for Hawaii. One of these is quite interesting and was released with a misspelling, "The Island of Oahu" spelled "Ohau." Twenty five thousand were struck before the error was discovered and new dies made for the remainder of the issues.

Medal of Captain James Cook

A coin collector and author, Clifford Mishler, struck medals to commemorate statehood in six different metals. All of these are now collectors' items.

Tokens

Actually, very few tokens were used on the Island and the situation was just the reverse of the Alaska one, where thousands of tokens and bingles were used, especially in the bars and saloons.

Among the tokens used in Hawaii are the plantation tokens which are scarce or rare. These come in 12-1/2¢, 1/2 Real, 1 Real, 6¢ or 1/2 Bit denominations. They were issued during the 1870's and 1880's, in most cases to pay laborers, and were accepted at company stores only. The two most famous plantations were the Haiku and the Waliluku.

Hawaiian Token, 1880
1/2 Real denomination

The Thomas H. Hobron Railroad token was issued in the 12-1/2¢ or two-bit denominations. When the Hobron Railroad was absorbed by the Kahului Railroad, tokens in the denominations of 10¢, 15¢ 20¢, 35¢, and 75¢ were issued. All of these railroad tokens are very scarce and in demand.

A very unusual numismatic item is a test striking of the Hobron Dies on an 1872 U. S. half-dollar. This piece is unique. It was in the author's collection for a number of years and is now in the famous Hawaiian collection of the Ostheimers of Honolulu, Hawaii.

One of the rarest tokens is the John P. Waterhouse piece issued in 1862. This token circulated throughout the Islands and was redeemed by Waterhouse at his dry goods store. The condition of many of these pieces indicates a good deal of circulation.

The Waterhouse token is an especially interesting piece because while most of the Hawaiian tokens have just a star or minor emblems on them, the obverse of this piece has the bust of His Majesty, Kamehameha IV, on it. The reverse depicts a beehive. This piece is eagerly sought by collectors.

There are some early saloon tokens that are scarce. Among the modern issues are those issued for school cafeterias, Department of Public Instruction, bakeries, and ice companies. There are a number of transportation tokens which were used at various times.

Hawaiian Token of John Waterhouse

Pattern or Trial Pieces

Of great interest are the Pattern or Trial coins of Queen Liliuokalani, issued to commemorate her reign in 1891 and 1893, which are among the most beautiful coins ever struck.

They were issued by Reginald Huth of England, a collector of coins and medals who struck a number of the private Pattern coins and other pieces. These items never went into circulation, but were kept as souvenirs by friends and admirers of the former Queen. The issues were extremely small, with from four to fifty pieces only struck, making them very rare.

Patterns were struck in the year 1881 by King Kalakaua. It is thought that the pieces were struck in Paris. Occasionally a worn piece is found, showing that somehow or other it got into circulation before it was recognized as being a Pattern or scarce item.

Charles Barber, who designed the regular issue of 1883 for the Government, also designed some of the 1883 Patterns with the 12-1/2¢ denomination, which were subsequently discarded.

In 1893, another Pattern dollar was struck in honor of Princess Kaiulani. This dollar is among the most attractive and desirable of all Hawaiian coins.

1847 *Hawaiian Pattern Cent in Pewter*

A most unusual discovery of one of the great rarities of Hawaiian numismatics was made a few years ago when a Hawaiian Pewter Pattern cent of 1847 made its appearance.

Until this cent was publicized, the only known pieces were the copper cents, listed in several varieties.

These copper cents were never popular or accepted by the natives and many of the pieces were thrown into the sea, mutilated, or destroyed. This was the only official copper coin for the Kingdom of Hawaii and approximately 100,000 of them were minted. The coins bear the head of King Kamehameha III on the obverse while the reverse has the legend in Hawaiian, "Kingdom of Hawaii," etc.

The pewter piece was discovered in a collection of coins assembled by a Mr. John Ellis of Melrose, Mass. Ellis' collection consisted of U. S. large cents, Indian Head cents, and rare tokens, all of which were tacked to a board—the custom among coin collectors in the 19th century. This kind of mounting accounts for the minor edge damage which appeared on the coin and the type of bruise familiar to most older collectors and dealers.

The collection did not come to light until after Ellis had been dead for more than seventy years, but the coins were still intact. Ellis had a friend who was a die sinker living in Belmont, Mass. It was he who made the regular Hawaiian cents of 1847, that were shipped to Hawaii.

Many years ago, the famed numismatist, Wayte Raymond, would go to Belmont to buy quantities of the Hawaiian cent from the die sinker or his heirs and the secret was kept well guarded.

The new discovery does not compare with any of the known varieties. It could not have been made for general circulation as the Law of 1846 authorizes the striking of the cent in copper only.

James J. Jarvis, who ordered the coins for the Hawaiian government, ran a general store and was editor of the newspaper, "Polynesian." The government gave him a note for $869.50 to cover the cost of the coins, and this was paid when the 100,000 cents were delivered.

When the coins arrived on January 14, 1847 the design was a great surprise to everyone in Honolulu. As stated previously, the coins were not at all popular and did not circulate freely. Consequently, no further orders for these cents were placed. This would account for the fact that one die, at least, was never used for minting.

Belt Buckle Dollar

The Hawaiian Silver Dollar of 1883 is an interesting and desirable coin. A collector from Clare, Michigan, wrote me about one of these dollars. In 1911, my correspondent had lived at Redondo Beach, California, where a Hawaiian band performed every evening. Being sixteen, and a fairly good billiard player, the young man was challenged to a game of pool one afternoon by a member of the band.

After losing a few dollars, the musician declared himself broke, except for a Hawaiian dollar which had been made into a brooch. He told his young opponent that in 1883 the King had the United States make up some silver coins at the San Francisco Mint. Arrangements were made for the King to pay the United States a certain amount each year, but his non-payment of debts eventually led to his downfall.

The musician went on to say that the King had made, at great expense, brooches out of two of the silver dollars; half of the silver was taken out of one reverse and half of the silver out of the other obverse, and each coin was then refinished with jade and jewels. These pieces were made by an English jeweler and were supposed to have been very expensive.

My correspondent adds that he still has the brooch which he won. The story goes that the other piece was pinned to the King when he was buried. The enamel work on the brooch is beautiful enough to mark it truly a distinctive work of art.

Finally, my Michigan correspondent states that he does not know whether the story is true and that he is now seventy years old and no longer playing pool.

I am sorry to say that from my own experience the story the musician told the young man could not possibly have been true. I have seen a number of these beautifully enamelled pieces which were used for various forms of jewelry, including belt buckles, pins and pendants. Other foreign silver dollars have been used for the same purpose and are quite attractive.

Stories of this sort are often heard by numismatists but

when checked thoroughly, they are usually found to have little truth, although there is a romance in them that is always intriguing.

The Odd and Curious Money of Alaska

Alaska has a fascinating history; it was under Russian rule until it was sold to the United States in 1867; and later gold was discovered leading to fabulous wealth coming out of its vast wilderness in the past hundred years. All this is a perfect background for a rich and varied coinage.

Alaska's towns and hamlets are dotted with saloons and general stores. Trading posts are to be found close to the borders of Siberia. In the far north Eskimos and polar bears roam. It was only natural that over the years the proprietors of these various establishments should issue tokens, especially during the periods when there was a shortage of change. These tokens are among the most important items in the study of Alaskan numismatics, and are called "Bingles."

Before the advent of the traders, the Eskimos used the barter and trading system. Among the items used by the Eskimos for trading were polar bear teeth and shark teeth (which were brought from the south by sailors) along with useful objects that could be of assistance in making their daily tasks easier. Trading and bartering with objects made of ivory was common also.

When the white traders arrived, they brought beads, blankets, and buttons which were much in demand for trading with the Indian and Eskimo natives. Trading beads were of various kinds, often beautifully colored. These are difficult to obtain since they are considered family heirlooms among the Indians. The Indian woman would bring her dowry of beads with her when married and to accumulate many strands of beads became a lifelong ambition.

The trading beads came from every corner of the world

which is why there are so many varieties to be found. At that time a large glass bead was worth an unbelievable number of animal skins, giving the traders very substantial profits on their northern journeys. The trips were both arduous and dangerous, but the financial return was most worthwhile.

Large wooden fishhooks, as well as items such as caribou and seal teeth, were highly prized by the Indians and are to be found in collections of "odd and curious" money.

One of the most unusual pieces of money is the so-called "Bread Money" of Alaska, which actually was bread, dried and dehydrated over a long period, that had practically turned to stone, and was then used as money.

In the years that Russia controlled Alaska through the Russian-American Company, sealskin notes were used. These had the denomination and name of the company printed on the sealskin. Very few specimens of these notes remain today. Some Russian coins did circulate, but actually the natives were just as happy to be paid in trade goods.

After the United States purchased Alaska from the Russians, there was very little activity until the famous gold strike brought thousands of people from all over the world to seek fortunes from the land. Some became permanent settlers, establishing towns and villages.

"The King of Alaskan Tokens" is the Valdez piece, which shows a gold nugget in its center. The obverse has the legend, "Native gold, Valdez, Alaska, Copper Block Buffet," and the reverse "Good for one dollar in merchandise." One dollar did not have much value in the gold rush days of 1898.

A great many tokens were issued at the turn of the century. Others, struck more recently, are still in use today.

At Gambell, the settlement nearest Russia, the Reindeer Commercial Company issued tokens in denominations up to $10. The N. C. Company, which is to Alaska what the

Hudson Bay Company is to Canada, also issued tokens in many denominations.

The Bingles of 1935, issued for use in the Matanuska Valley Colonization Project, are the only U. S. Government tokens authorized for use in Alaska. (There were no coins minted for actual circulation by any government at any period of Alaskan history.)

The 1935 tokens were backed and issued by the U. S. Government's Alaska Rural Rehabilitation Corporation.

In the spring of 1935, the Federal Government, trying to relieve the hardships of farmers in the drought-stricken areas of the middle west, shipped 201 settlers to the fertile Matanuska Valley, in Alaska. A hundred and twenty men, taken from relief rolls, were sent ahead to clear land and make other preparations for the settlers, so that the families would have some temporary dwellings available on arrival.

The first settlers arrived in Palmer in 1935. They were followed by families from Michigan and Wisconsin. Each family was alloted a forty acre plot.

From the beginning, there was dissatisfaction among the settlers. Quarrels with administrative officials, homesickness and complaints of having been misinformed about the prospects in the area reached such proportions that after a stay of only a few months, some of the group returned to the United States.

Of the original 201 settlers, 66 families departed, leaving only a small portion of the pioneer group. The colonization experiment was deemed unsuccessful even though some of the original settlers have remained to this day.

Alaska A.R.R.C. "Bingles" were issued in 1935 and could be spent only at the Government Commissary or A.R.R.C. stores, but merchants, including the local saloon keepers, accepted the tokens, and though the chief purpose of the tokens was to keep the workers from spending their money unwisely, the government had no choice but to withdraw the tokens from circulation and to replace them with regular U. S. coins.

The tokens were struck in small quantities of 1,000 to 5,000 pieces, in denominations from 1¢ to $10.

It is said that some of the $5 and $10 Bingles were holed and used for washers and in other odd ways, thus destroying them from a numismatic viewpoint. These denominations are already rare and will become increasingly difficult to obtain in the future. The majority of these pieces were destroyed. There are only 250 sets in existence.

One of the scarce tokens in the 10¢ denomination can be obtained for around $25. Complete sets catalog from $400 to $500.

* * *

A twelve-year-old Waltham, Massachusetts, youth made one of the most unusual of recent numismatic finds. Jonathan D. Furbush, an alert, bright youngster, always interested in the unusual, came upon the rare numismatic treasure in the following manner. The Furbushes, an old Massachusetts family, had an area on their estate which at one time had been Jonathan's great-grandfather's apple orchard. A new roadway had been brought through this land, very near the Furbush home. In the course of the construction, Jonathan spent every spare moment watching as each new shovelful of earth was turned.

One day, he noticed a shiny object. On picking it up, he at first thought it to be an old coin. After taking it home and removing the surface dirt, he found it to be an attractive piece, and kept it out of curiosity. Although he was interested in the item, he attached no particular importance to it. He showed it to his father, who checked it with several friends interested in numismatics. They suggested the piece be further checked out.

Alaskan Token discovered by a young Massachusetts collector

When this was done, the piece was found to be a Unique and Rare token of Alaska. The obverse has the following legend: "Anchorage, Alaska, Native Virgin Gold and Copper," and has a gold nugget in the center. It also has the letters "Val" under the gold nugget, which may refer to the town of Valdez, which is noted for its gold and copper mines.

The reverse also is very unusual and has the national resources of Alaska listed, as follows: "Gold, Copper, Coal, Fish, Lumber, Dairy, Livestock, Agriculture." In the center the midnight sun is depicted beside a glacier, with the legend, "Midnight Sun."

This piece survived the elements of the tough New England climate for many years and is in an excellent state of preservation.

One wonders how an Alaskan token happened to be buried in New England soil. Did a returning miner, who might have helped pick apples in Jonathan's great-grandfather's orchard, lose his lucky token? Possibly the Furbush family will some day find in its records the information that one of its members visited or mined in Alaska and brought back this long-lost find.

* * *

The story of Talkeetna, originally an Indian settlement that remains a small, unincorporated village, was told to Joe Crusey, researcher and numismatist, by the son of an old Alaska settler.

With no organized government in this village settlement, the only representative of legal authority was a U. S. Marshall who was eventually moved to Seward, leaving only the U. S. Commissioner as representative of law and order.

When the Alaska railroad came through the area, Talkeetna, being one of the stops, became the nearest rail link to travel into the Cashe Creek mining district. Because of this, settlers from Susitna, which did not have railroad connections, moved up the river. The 1940 census of the entire area shows a population of only three hundred.

H. W. Nagley arrived in this area in the early 1920's to start a General Store. For a time, the store was nothing more than business in a tent on Nagley Street. Eventually, Mr. Nagley expanded his business interests to include restaurants, furnished rooms, liquor, and game tables for cards and pool. In addition to his various commercial ventures, Nagley was U. S. Commissioner for a considerable period in the 1930's.

To encourage trade at a time when there was a shortage of money and coins, Bingles were made up. The only cost to the issuer was the cost of manufacture and the Bingles were almost always redeemed for merchandise or in trade. These tokens, good at H. W. Nagley's store and other operations, encouraged trading with his enterprises. Used in card games and at the pool tables these tokens stimulated business for the Nagley-owned enterprises since they were not generally acceptable at a competitor's place of business.

Bingles were also issued by B. N. Nauman's, a similar Talkeetna establishment which is now known as The Fairview Inn.

The Nagley Bingles were of 25¢ and 50¢ denominations, but Mr. Nagley recalls that at one time 12-1/2¢ denominations were used in Talkeetna.

After Nagley's roadhouse was sold, the use of the Bingles was discontinued. Whenever they were brought in, they could be exchanged for money or—preferably—merchandise at the H. W. Nagley store. Tokens were not used by H. W. Nagley in Susitna. Nagley, Sr. retired and moved to Seattle, Washington. The tokens he issued in Talkeetna, Alaska have added much numismatic color to the history of the Territory.

Another token issued about 1935, by Oscar Samuelsen of Bethel, was used at Samuelsen's Trading Post to buy furs and fish from the natives. Bethel had a population of approximately 400 people and four large trading posts, which served about 2,000 people—mostly natives and a sprinkling of immigrant trappers and fishermen.

At Mt. Village, the Shepards issued tokens in 25¢, 50¢, $1, $5, $10 and $20 denominations. That Bingles were seldom issued at values lower than 25¢ indicates there was little need for small change. The $20 denomination on the other hand is fairly high for this medium of exchange.

At one time the Government ordered Shepard to discontinue the circulation of his tokens since operating in a real outpost like Mt. Village gave him a virtual monopoly on all the commerce and trading in his area if he should refuse to deal in cash.

Traders showed considerable ingenuity and shrewdness in their use of these tokens, for it enabled them to keep cash and insured them a continuous trade with those who had

Set of Alaska Tokens of the Sheppard Trading Company

received the Bingles.

Alaskan coins and tokens are becoming increasingly popular with collectors, who are attracted to the series by the colorful and exciting history of barter and coinage of one of the newest of the United States.

Puerto Rico

The commonwealth of Puerto Rico, with close ties to the United States—and a possible fifty-first state some day—is of considerable interest to U. S. coin collectors.

The island, discovered by Christopher Columbus in 1493, has a history of war, privateers, pirates, and revolution.

Puerto Rico was ceded to the United States in 1898, after

the Spanish-American War. American citizenship was granted to the Puerto Rican people in 1917.

The numismatic history of Puerto Rico appeals to student and collector, encompassing, as it does, the early Cob and Pillar pieces, and the Hacienda tokens, once popular on the island. The Cob pieces take their name from the Spanish words *Cabo de Barra* which mean, quite literally, "end of the bar." These early silver pieces were very crudely made by a primitive method. A chunk of silver was cut from the end of the bar and struck by hand dies to mint the coin. Because of the hand minting the coins are irregular and poorly struck.

Puerto Rico used the same Spanish Colonial coins that circulated all over North and South America. Pieces of eight and the doubloons of pirate fame circulated along with the other Spanish Colonial pieces.

Fleur-de-Lis Counterstamp used in Puerto Rico struck on United States Liberty Seated Quarter

In 1857 (the same year that the United States demonetized the Spanish Colonial coins), all of the crude silver Cob coins were ordered withdrawn from circulation in Puerto Rico. At that time, Mexican, British, French, and United States coins were all circulating on the Island.

During the 1870's, there was a serious shortage of coins. Coins then in circulation were "holed" to keep them from being taken off the island. A law was passed requiring all the holed coins to be counterstamped with a *fleur-de-lis*. These pieces, now collectors' items, include many varieties of coins, including U. S. silver dollars, trade dollars, half-dollars, quarters, twenty cent pieces, Spanish silver, and even a few copper and bronze pieces. Being scarce, these pieces are eagerly sought now by both counterstamp and type collectors.

The only regular Puerto Rican coinage was issued in 1895 and 1896. The peso, or dollar size coin, was struck in 1895, with a mintage of 8,500,000. The 1896 40 centavos had 725,000 minted. The 20 centavos was struck in 1895 and 967,000 were minted. The 10 centavos, struck in 1896, had 700,000 minted. 600,000 of the 1896 5 centavo were minted.

All of these coins were struck in silver. They are more

Puerto Rican Pattern or Trial Piece of 1890
This piece was never accepted and is a real collector's item.

scarce than the mintage would indicate because over the years, innumerable coins have been mutilated and used for jewelry. Since it is a small, thin, silver coin, the 5 centavos especially is often found on bracelets and other kinds of jewelry.

Puerto Rican Tokens

The largest series of numismatic items are the tokens of Puerto Rico. Of unusual interest are the Plantation or Hacienda tokens, which were most frequently issued in the 1880's and 1890's as wages to the workers on the plantations. Circulated widely, these tokens were accepted by both local merchants and the company stores as exchange for goods.

When the merchants had accumulated enough tokens, they would send them back to the plantation or hacienda owners for redemption. It is amazing that none of these tokens were unredeemed or not honored for cash.

More than 250 varieties are now known and new ones will undoubtedly continue to come to light from time to time. These tokens come in various metals: brass, copper,, bronze, nickel, aluminum, tin, etc.

The denominations for most of these tokens are given in *Almudes,* the *Almuda* being a unit of measure for coffee used by the coffee pickers. Other tokens used were centavos, reales, and Jornaldiario.

Many of the pieces are counterstamped, some very crudely. One unusual piece has an eight-pointed star and various Masonic symbols. These were worth 25% more than the unstamped varieties.

The tokens of the Hacienda Mercedita were sometimes cut into quarters for use as small change.

Many denominations were used, including: 6-1/4 centavos, 12-1/2 centavos, 1 cent, 4 reales, 1/2 reale, 3 reales, 4 centavos.

In 1882 the Hacienda de Miguel Marquez Y Ensenat had

5, 6, 7, and 8 Almudes. The obverse of this very attractive piece has a radiant sun in a circle of dots. The reverse displays the particular denomination.

Some of the tokens are just pieces of metal bearing crude counterstamps. The S. Alvarado, Aguadilla token has no denomination on it.

Puerto Rican tokens, popular with collectors as are the tokens of Canada, Alaska, the Virgin Islands, and Mexico, are now considered an important part of the numismatics of the Americas.

Paper Money of Puerto Rico

There is a small series of paper money issued for Puerto Rico, all of which is considered scarce or rare, except the Billete de Canje notes.

These were bills of exchange, with a value of 1 peso, under the Decree of August 17, 1895, originally issued in books containing full sheets of notes. This was also done to detect counterfeits, since the notes were detached from the stubs with a special knife that left a wavy edge. This allowed the notes to be compared with the stubs, according to serial number and the way in which the edge was cut.

Some of the pieces can still be found with the original counterfoil and stub, some with the counterfoil, and others with neither counterfoil or stub.

Among the rare pieces are the 8 reals note of 1813 Tesoreria Nacional de Puerto Rico, a crude note which is very rare. Also rare are the 3 peso and 5 peso notes of 1815, which were issued by the Royal Treasury of Puerto Rico to pay the bearer in coin under guarantee of the taxes of the islands. These notes look a great deal like the early American broken banknotes of the 1815 period. Since they are very seldom offered, either for private sale or at auction, it is difficult to price these.

Among other interesting notes are those issued by the Railroad Company of Puerto Rico which were good for 5 pesos in silver Mexican coins to be paid the bearer upon presentation at the cashier's office of the Railroad Company. These notes, printed in London, were probably issued during the 1880's.

The Banco Espanol de Puerto Rico issued notes from 1896 to 1900. The two denominations known are 5 peso and 10 peso. An unusual feature of the 1900 5 peso is the overprint "Moneda Americana," meaning, "American Money."

In 1904, the Bank of Puerto Rico issued a 5 peso note with the inscription in both English and Spanish. All of these pieces are rare. In 1909 the same bank issued a $10 note of which the only known piece is in poor condition.

The most unusual note is one issued in 1869 by the authority of Republican Central Council of Cuba and Puerto Rico, which states it is indebted to the bearer in the amount of 1 peso. These notes, when presented in amounts of more than 100 pesos to the Treasury and the Council, were convertible into bonds of the Republic of Cuba.

1 peso and 5 peso denomination notes are known to have been issued in New York by the revolutionary organization called the Republican Central Council of Cuba and Puerto Rico. The notes were not legal tender in Puerto Rico and were never circulated on the Island.

National bank notes were issued by the First National Bank of Puerto Rico in San Juan, series of 1902, red seal, in the following denominations: $5, $10, $20, $50, and $100.

Also issued in 1902 were blue seal notes with dates from 1902 to 1908 on the reverse. These come in the same denominations as the red seal.

All of these notes are rare. Some are extremely rare.

It is expected that there will be new discoveries in the

numismatics of Puerto Rico as more Hacienda tokens and new paper money comes to light as a result of research now under way.

A collection of Puerto Rican material starting from the early 1500's and encompassing all of the coins from the crude Cob pieces and Pillar dollars to the coinage of 1895 and 1896 would be one of the most interesting in all the North American area.

Today the regular U. S. coinage is used on the Island and I have been told by visitors and servicemen who have been stationed there, that in some of the smaller towns many of the Barber dimes, quarters, and half-dollars dated 1892 to 1916 still circulate.

If it should happen that Puerto Rico becomes the 51st of the United States, Puerto Rican numismatic material would pyramid in value, as Hawaiian and Alaskan series have.

The Mystery of the Clay Faces

Many stories are told of the early uses of mediums of exchange. One that rivals the fascinating lore of pirate money or Wampum, is the story of the small human Clay Faces of Puerto Rico.

Howard Gibbs, one of the world's leading authorities on odd and curious money, was first introduced to these faces by a strange woman who came to him at a convention of the American Numismatic Association where he was exhibiting his collection of odd and curious money.

She showed him some unusual looking clay pieces and said they had been given to her by a U. S. Army colonel who had been stationed in Puerto Rico. He had told her the pieces had been used as money in the early days.

The island was originally peopled by the Borinqueno Indians, who were enslaved by the Spanish who conquered Puerto Rico in 1509. The Borinqueno—except for a few who escaped to other islands—were gradually exterminated as a result of the hardship of forced labor.

The story of the Clay Faces used as money in Puerto Rico is ghoulish and weird. They are still being found by people digging graves or working in the fields.

Perhaps they were impressions of gods or caricatures of idols. They may even have been symbolic of the rain, the wind, the heavens, and the sun. Possibly, they were dug out of clay pits in the hills and fashioned into faces representing figures from ancient native superstitions.

Another mysterious part of the story is the woman who left these curiosities with Gibbs for when he subsequently tried to trace her, it was as if she had never existed. All his efforts were futile, until finally he learned that she had been killed in an automobile accident immediately after she had left him at the hotel. It was as if whatever spirit had guided her to the hotel with those strange human Clay Faces, had also determined that she would never return.

Many years have passed and while nothing new has been found to substantiate the story of the human Clay Faces, they do exist. Did they belong to one of the many tribes? Were they used only in local areas or could they have been used as actual legal tender of the time? If so, why has the complete story never come to light?

Virgin Islands of the United States

A group of islands in the West Indies, commonly known as The Virgin Islands of the United States, and formerly the Danish West Indies, is situated as an outpost of the United States, in a position to furnish protection to the U. S. holdings in the Caribbean Sea and the Panama Canal.

Denmark colonized St. Thomas in 1666 and until 1755, the Danish West India Company controlled the Islands. In 1755, Frederik V of Denmark purchased the islands from the company. St. Thomas was declared a free port in 1764. In 1800, during the Napoleonic Wars, England blockaded St. Thomas, and in the year 1801, occupied the island. In 1802, St. Thomas was returned to Denmark, but then from 1807 to 1815, England occupied the Danish West Indies. In 1917, after negotiations begun prior to 1867, the United States purchased the Danish West Indies for $25,000,000.

The chief industries include fueling and servicing ships, manufacturing rum, fishing, cattle raising, and truck gardening. There is a large tourist industry which continues to grow and flourish.

The Danish West India Company struck the first coins for the islands, gold 2 ducat pieces, dated 1708. These are very rare, with only a few specimens known.

In 1849, 2 ducat and 1 ducat gold pieces were minted. These pieces were not for general circulation, being more in the nature of commemorative or presentation pieces. They are also considered rare.

In 1734, there existed a shortage of hard currency and King Christian VI gave permission for the Danish West India Company to have coins struck. Coins in denominations of 1 skilling, 2 skilling and 12 skilling were minted in Copenhagen and shipped to the West Indies.

Ships from many ports touched at the seaports in the area and consequently, many of these coins changed hands and were carried all over the world. The coin shortage became a phenomenon common to the other West Indies islands and seaports and in 1757, pieces were struck in the 12 skilling denomination. A short time later, between 1763 and 1767, at the end of the reign of Frederik V, a new coinage of 12 and 24 skilling pieces was issued. The 6 skilling and 12 skilling denominations were struck in 1782, though all bear the date 1767. These early coins were usually poorly struck and are difficult to find in sharp condition.

Between 1808 and 1839, during the reign of Frederik VI, 2 skilling, 10 skilling, and 20 skilling coins were struck. The designs on these coins were continued until 1848. Many of these were melted down at that time when the price of silver took a sharp rise above the bullion value and just about every bit of silver on the island was melted.

In 1848, Frederik VII authorized the striking of 2 skilling, 10 skilling, and 20 skilling pieces. All of the coins struck from 1816 to 1848 were well struck and are obtainable in sharp condition and known in Uncirculated and Proof condition.

It was also during this period that large numbers of foreign —including U. S.—coins were imported into the island and counterstamped with the famous Crown FR V that made them legal tender on the island. These counterstamped pieces are very desirable, especially the United States coins. The dollar-size coins are the most valuable. The large cent, in my opinion, is the most common.

In 1905, coins with two denominations on them were issued. The half-cent of 1905 is also marked "2-1/2 bit." The one cent, "5 bit," the two cent, "10 bit" and the five cent, "25 bit," as well as the ten cent, which was "50 bit."

In great demand are the 4 daler and 10 daler gold of 1904 and 1905. These pieces bring higher prices every time they are offered for sale or at auction.

Tokens of the Virgin Islands

One of the most historically interesting series is the Merchants Tokens which were issued between 1888 and 1892.

Among the denominations used were: 1 centavo, 3, 5, and 10 centavo and 1, 3, 5, and 10 cents. The centavo denomination was used because of the great many Mexican pesos circulated on the island. Many of the pieces have "Mexic." beside the denomination.

These pieces were struck in German silver, brass, and copper. There is no doubt that they actually circulated freely as currency. I have seen many of them worn. None of these are common and they become more difficult to obtain every year.

Paper Money of the Virgin Islands

The paper money of the Danish West Indies is rare in all of the early issues. There is a 1788 20 Rigsdaler, West Indies Currency Credit note, which is in the Royal Collection of Coins and Medals in Copenhagen, where they also have a 5 Rigsdaler note of 1822.

This kind of note was issued from 1788 to 1836 in denominations of 5, 10, 20, 50, and 100 Rigsdaler. The condition of most of these notes known is Fair to Poor. There is a 100 Rigsdaler Note issued in 1842 on which the printing is more modern. This issue also includes 5, 10, and 50 Rigsdaler denominations.

In 1849, the Danish West Indian dollar was placed on a par with the U. S. dollar and some notes were issued in $2, $3, $5, $10, $50, and 100 dollar denominations. The same series issued a $2 note dated 1860, and also 1898.

In 1905, the National Bank of the Danish West Indies issued notes in denominations of 5, 10, 20 and 100 francs. These notes, showing scenes from the island, the obverse of the note also picturing the king, are beautifully engraved. They are printed in both English and Danish and are gold certificates.

* * *

The popularity of this series will follow the same lines as that attained by Hawaii, Alaska, Puerto Rico, and the Philippines and will continue to be in demand for many years to come.

With approximately three hundred items to be obtained to complete a collection, either a type collection or general collection may be built up at the present time, but research done over the years will undoubtedly bring new tokens and varieties to light.

Revolutionary Coins of Cuba

In 1897, the Cuban Revolutionary Junta, with headquarters in New York City, struck the famous piece known as the Cuban Souvenir Peso.

There were three distinct die types for this dollar-size coin minted to raise money and create publicity for the cause named The Liberation and Establishment of a Free Cuba.

In 1898, a small number of pieces were struck. These are very rare.

In 1897, 9,970 specimens were struck in the three varieties. These items proved to be very popular and are now found in collections all over the world.

In 1965, history repeated itself when a group called The Agency for Cuban Numismatics in Exile, with the backing of Alpha 66 (11 Frente-Alpha 66-M.R.P.)—a leading Cuban Revolutionary group, having a long and sustained action against Castro's tyranny—issued another Souvenir coin dated 1965.

While these pieces closely resemble the items struck in 1897, a few significant changes were added.

The obverse bears a youthful head of Liberty facing right, giving the date, 19-65, with the motto "Patria Y Libertad" above, and the word "Souvenir" below.

The reverse, following the original, uses the central design of the Cuban Coat of Arms, but with the legend "Cubanos En Exilio" (Cubans in Exile) divided by two small stars from the fineness, 925-Fino, with six stars below.

It was originally planned to strike the same number of pieces that had been minted in 1897, but because of various difficulties, only half that number was struck, leaving the issue a very small one.

These dollar-size coins were made available in luxurious leatherette cases decorated with the Cuban Coat of Arms on the outside and the colors of the Cuban flag on the inside.

A group of numismatists, who left Cuba during the Castro regime, formed a collectors' group called The Cuban Numismatic Society in Exile, with Luis F. Ardois as its President. This group considers the Revolutionary piece not to be a regular coin or issued under official sanction and disowns it, even though part of the proceeds was to go to Alpha 66 for use by the revolutionary group in its crusade against Castro's Communist regime.

There will be a great deal of controversy about this item for many years to come, but because of the small mintage and its association, it will find its way into private collections and museums as well.

No one knows what the future will hold in Cuban numismatics, but there is a chance that many of the silver pieces will become rare, especially the dollar-size pieces, most of which were melted by the Cuban government when the price of silver rose in 1948. This also applies to all other Cuban gold and silver coins, all of which were recalled from circulation in 1961, melted, and made into bars, which were eventually sent to Russia in payment for arms and military supplies.

VI

∎

Some Numismatic Stories
The Coin Spins A Tale

The Ugly Head

Have any of you heard of the word "ugly" applied to George Washington, "father of our country?"

"The Ugly Head" is one of the most unusual and rare Washington medals. The portrait on this satirical medal is in profile and shows Washington with his wig off and his false teeth removed. Furthering the grotesque appearance is the unflattering and abnormal expression of the features. It is, indeed, an "Ugly Head."

The medal's reverse has a chain of 13 rings, each bearing the name of one of the original 13 Colonies, and in the center space, the figures "84," probably for the year 1784.

Washington Ugly Head
A famous satirical piece

The obverse, or face of the medal, has the legend, WASHINGTON THE GREAT, D. G., with the very Ugly Head facing right.

As a military leader, Washington drove the British from Boston on March 17, 1776; defeated the Hessian troops at Trenton, December 25, 1776; and expelled the British from Princeton on January 3, 1777. He also succeeded, against great odds, in holding together the Continental Army at Valley Forge during the bitter winters of 1777 and 1778.

He is depicted in famous paintings and drawings as being of regal and refined bearing. His aristocratic features have been portrayed by many famous artists.

Little is known about the origin of The Ugly Head. The few specimens that have come to light have been discovered in and near Boston.

While there has been much speculation about this item, my own research leads me to believe that the following story could explain its existence.

A group of Tories, still bitter over defeat by Washington's army, were preparing to leave for Canada where they could continue to live under the sovereignty of King George III. Before departing, however, they wanted to do everything possible to belittle the great hero of the American Revolution. A small band of these die-hards were seated around a table at Beacon Hill, berating General Washington, when one of the men suggested striking a medal that would hold Washington up to ridicule. It was decided to strike the piece that we now call The Ugly Head.

The pieces were struck and distributed in a surreptitious manner. When patriotic Americans obtained any of the medals, they destroyed them, but the Tories probably kept them. I believe that some day one or two pieces will come to light in Canada.

One of these medals is in the national collection at the

Smithsonian Institute, Washington, D. C.; one at the museum of the Massachusetts Historical Society in Boston. Another is in my own collection. A few other Ugly Heads are known to exist.

All major coin publications list this piece as "Extremely Rare" and it was pictured for the first time only a few years ago. None of these pieces has been offered either for private sale or at auction for a great many years, but there is no doubt that one would bring a fabulous price since a great many museums and historical societies would enthusiastically welcome such a rarity—and so would private collectors of coins and medals.

Another extremely interesting Washington medal is the Washington Funeral Medal. This was struck in several metals and is rare. Funeral Medals usually come holed, as they were worn by those who participated in Washington's funeral parade.

The King of American Coins

The title "King of American Coins" applies to the 1804 U. S. Silver Dollar.

Over the years sensational stories and articles concerning this historical piece have appeared and intrigued both the collector and the public. One story tells of a shipment of the 1804 Silver Dollars being sent to Tripoli to take care of America's financial needs in the war against the pirates. According to the story, the ship was sunk with most of the coins on board.

Another story relates that a large shipment was stolen in transit and buried somewhere in Texas or California.

These are only two of the many tall tales that have persisted through the years, perhaps gaining embellishments and added touches from time to time.

The mint records show that 19,570 silver dollars were coined in 1804, but it is known that these figures are incorrect. There are fifteen pedigreed specimens known of this coin.

Occasionally a new story appears or a collector claims to have found another 1804 silver dollar, but when checked out, the coins are usually found to be altered dates cleverly retooled to resemble the original.

In 1875, one of these dollars sold for $325, a big price for the period. In 1876, one of the 1804 coins realized a price of $500. From then until now, the price has risen steadily. At a public auction in 1960, one of these rarities brought $28,000 and at another auction in 1961, $29,000 was the price realized. The chances are that when another one appears on the market, new records will be set.

There may be one that you can examine in your part of the country, since some of these items are owned by institutions and museums. You can see "The King of American Coins" on display at the Chase Manhattan Money Museum in New York City; Johns Hopkins University, Baltimore, Maryland; the National Collection at the Smithsonian Institute, Washington, D. C.; in the collection of the Omaha Public Library at Omaha, Nebraska; and at the Massachusetts Historical Society in Boston, Massachusetts.

It is quite a thrill to see or handle one of the most sought-after coins in the world.

Some students of numismatics do not class this piece as a coin of the regular U. S. series because research has shown is was struck at a period later than it was dated.

Controversies and arguments about this famous coin will continue, no doubt, through the years, but in spite of this, the 1804 silver dollar will continue to be the "King of American Coins."

1804 Silver Dollar
One of the world's most valuable coins

The Maximilian Peso

The Maximilian Peso or dollar is one of the most sought Mexican coins.

Maximilian reigned as the Emperor of Mexico for a short period between 1864 and 1867.

When the last coinage was struck during his reign, the die broke and the last piece was badly mangled. It was difficult to see any resemblance to a dollar. This piece was saved by one of the workmen, who subsequently presented it to the Empress Carlotta as a souvenir of the incident.

On examination of some of the coins, it was discovered that when the die was first broken, a small clip appeared like a gash on the forehead of Maximilian. The crack appeared larger in each of thirty-two pieces, and then in the thirty-third, thirty-fourth, and thirty-fifth pieces became badly broken. The thirty-sixth was the badly mangled piece of silver that was presented to the Empress.

When this discovery was first made, some of the workmen thought that it might be an omen of disaster. When they found out that Maximilian had been thirty-two years old when he became Emperor of Mexico and realized that he was then in the third year of his reign, the superstitious among them believed that the badly mangled thirty-sixth piece indicated some tragic impending disaster. As the fears of the workmen mounted the frightening story became further embellished as it went from one person to another.

An American officer was in charge of the mint at that time. He immediately secured the broken dollar pieces.

The Emperor Ferdinand Joseph Maximilian had been on the Mexican throne for three years and one week when he was executed on June 19, 1867, at the age of thirty-six.

One of the most unusual circumstances was that the Emperor's body was mangled and that one bullet entered his head at the exact spot shown by the gash on the silver dollar.

In the early 1870's one of the gashed coins came into the possession of Dr. I. E. Nagle, of Mt. Joy, Pennsylvania. His story was published in the Philadelphia newspapers, as well as in the *American Journal of Numismatics* and it provoked a great deal of interest.

I have written and spoken to many collectors of old Mexican coins, but even those who have handled a great many of the Maximilian dollars have never seen one with the described broken die mark.

Perhaps with this story revealed again, someone, somewhere, has one of these interesting pieces put away among his mutilated coins, not knowing the tremendous historical significance of this unusual item. Mexican history is replete with many anecdotes pertaining to the unusual in numismatics.

The Lundy Puffin

The lonely Island of Lundy off the English coast was purchased for 6,000 pounds by a London financier, Martin Coles Harman. This island had a history of independence going back to the days of the pirates and invaders and was secluded for many centuries. Mr. Harman did not wish to develop or commercialize the island but to preserve its ancient way of life.

Two of the most interesting coins ever struck were the Lundy Puffin coins. There were several reasons that prompted Harman to issue them. The puffin bird nests on this island and has figured in many designs of stamps, pottery, and souvenirs sold there. Harman ordered two coins in denominations of ½ Puffin and 1 Puffin.

The obverse showed a likeness of Harman with the legend, MARTIN COLES HARMAN, 1929. The reverse showed a puffin with the legend LUNDY and the denomination.

These coins created a furor in England and in 1930 Harman was prosecuted by the British government and convicted of unlawfully issuing coins, which is prohibited by Section 5 of the Coinage Act of 1870. He was fined 5 pounds and ordered to pay costs. An appeal was filed, but it was dismissed by the Lord Chief Justice.

An unusual element of the story is that no order was issued to confiscate the puffin tokens and they remained on sale on the island until the supply was sold out.

Harman himself had designed the coins, of which 50,000 of each denomination were produced. Workmen were paid in Puffins which were used for general business on the island.

Colonial Curiosities

A blot on America's early Colonial history was the justice meted out at the Salem Witch Trials in the 1690's. Much fear and superstition accompanied the "witch hunt." Most of the details are common knowledge today.

A popular belief of the period was that wearing a bent coin protected one from the witches' evil powers. This is the reason many of the early Pine Tree and Oak Tree shillings come with holes and ridges where the coins had once been bent.

In some cases, tooth marks show, since it was possible to bend the thin coins very easily. I have noticed tooth marks, but not dents, on some of the early Pine Tree coins. I believe these were holed for suspension and used as infants' teething rings in Colonial days.

World's Largest Metal Coin

The world's largest metal coin was minted in Sweden in 1644. This tremendous coin measures 14"x24." It is one half inch thick, and weighs 44 pounds. This piece, a 10 daler denomination, had a value equivalent to two cows. These

The world's largest coin. Minted in Sweden in 1644 this copper coin measures 14x24 inches, one-half inch thick and weights 44 pounds.

pieces are called Plate Money. Their weight made it difficult to steal them.

In 1619, one of Europe's oldest companies, the Avesta Steel Company, first obtained a monolopy to refine, mint, and sell copper coins. Avesta produced all Swedish copper coins until 1831.

There are only three of the 10 daler coins in existence today. Many collectors, as well as the public, had an opportunity to view of these unusual pieces on exhibition at the 1964-1965 New York World's Fair.

Ho! For Idaho

An unusual piece of paper money from the early years of the American west is the $10 note of the First National Bank of Idaho, Boise City, Idaho Territory.

This note is beautifully engraved, with scenes of the old west, quartz tunneling, and a bust of General Ulysses S. Grant. It was issued in the 1860's. The reverse has an unusual caption—HO! FOR IDAHO. Some early public relations expert must have had a hand in designing this note, for it has considerable local advertising value. Evidently some group wanted to give Idaho a commercial plug on its currency.

Playing Card Money

Playing card money, circulated in French Canada from 1685 to 1759, is among the most interesting medium of exchange used on the North American continent.

During the early Colonial period, currency of many countries—Portugal, Mexico, Spain, and France—circulated in North America.

Because of the scarcity of currency and coinage, the French Colonial authorities issued playing card money in 1685. Originally issued as a temporary measure to help the merchants at a difficult time, this money was made by cutting playing cards in quarters which, after being affixed with the seal of the treasurer in wax, were signed by the governor.

The first issue was in denomination of 15 sols, 40 sols, and 4 francs. A little later, a quarter of a card, half a card, or a whole card was used for different denominations.

Originally intended only for a brief emergency period, these cards were circulated and accepted by the people, and remained an important part of the currency of French Canada until the fall of Quebec in 1759.

The Emperors of Kutch

An unusual coin situation existed in India in the state of Kutch during 1936 when in the same year coins were issued honoring three British monarch—George V, Edward VIII, and George VI. A set of these interesting 5 Koris silver pieces sells for approximately $250.

Anti-Banking Bills

The history of paper money in the Unites States is rife with stories of speculation, fraud, and misrepresentation, partly because the U. S. Government had no laws pertaining to the issuing of paper money by private banking firms and other non-government-affiliated companies.

The following episode allegedly took place in 1836 when the financial resources of the Mormons were at low ebb, and at a time when most of the Mormons were located in the town of Kirkland, Ohio.

Mormon prophet Joseph Smith, received a timely revelation commanding the establishment of the Kirkland Safety Society Anti-Banking Company. Ohio law at that time provided that all notes, bills, bonds, and other securities of an unchartered bank be held in the courts as absolutely void. This law did not deter Smith from organizing the Kirkland Safety Society Bank with a purported capital of $4,000,000.

Articles of agreement were drawn up on November 2, 1836, and Oliver Cowdery was sent to Philadelphia to obtain printing plates so that notes could be produced.

Another envoy, Orson Hyde, set out for the state capital to secure a charter for the bank, but the application was refused. Meanwhile, Cowdery took no chance of failure on his mission and came back to Kirkland, not only with the plates, but with $200,000 in printed bills.

"Anti-Banking" was used in the name of the company in an effort to keep these bills within the laws of the state of Ohio.

The Mormon Elders were sent out into the country to barter off the Kirkland money, which they undertook to do with great zeal, continuing the operation until the notes dropped to 12-1/2¢ on the dollar. Some of the notes were disposed of in Canada where the bank's credit was good.

This kind of enterprise was not uncommon during that period. Other companies used the same methods and prices of notes fluctuated, in accordance with the part of the country they were in and the willingness of other banks and companies to accept them.

Joseph Smith was accused by one of his former disciples, Cyrus Smolley of duping Mormons and others alike in the bank's organization. Smolley claimed to have been involved in this affair and said that he wanted to expose his former accomplices and their dealings. "Smith had 200 boxes made and filled them with lead and shot and marked them '$1000' each," Smolley related. "When people came to the bank's vaults to examine the assets, he showed them the boxes and told them the church had $200,000 in specie in the boxes. He opened one box, which was partly filled with silver, and after showing it to them, they would go away satisfied."

Smith's banking and commercial enterprises had disastrous results. His circulatory medium had no redeeming basis and was worthless in the hands of the people.

In 1838, Smith and Rigdon, being at Kirkland together, were both arrested on charges of swindling in connection with their worthless paper notes and other fraudulent operations.

The prisoners escaped the sheriff during the night and made their way on horesback to Missouri.

One must remember that at that time the Mormons were persecuted, looked upon as foreigners, and driven from place to place until they finally settled in their "promised land" in Utah.

The Kirkland Society notes are now quite rare and are signed by the highest dignitaries of the Mormon church, including Smith, Rigdon, and other leaders of the period.

The Moulton Copper

All New Hampshire Colonial coins are very rare and the rarest is the Wm. Moulton Copper of 1776.

The first piece was discovered in Portsmouth, New Hampshire, in 1875, by a laborer, who, when removing a bank of earth, discovered an interesting coin. The discoverer refused to part with it for many years, asking a price so high that no buyers who would meet it could be found.

The coin had a Pine Tree with the year 1776 on the obverse and the reverse legend read, LIBERTY AMERICAN, with the initials WM in the center. The initials WM stood for Wm. Moulton who was empowered by the state of New Hampshire to make copper coins to meet the need for small change in the Colonies.

It was almost ninety years later before another Wm. Moulton piece came to light. Frank D. Washburn and I discovered it in checking an old collection of coins that had originally belonged to a New Hampshire doctor. Then only a few years later, another piece came into a coin shop in the Boston area and was authenticated, making three pieces now known.

The original piece is now in the Johns Hopkins Museum and the other two pieces are in private collections.

I last saw one of these pieces priced at $10,000, and it will probably bring higher prices in the future.

If two pieces have come to light recently, there is always a possibility that one or two more of these coins is floating around in some old button box, or tucked away in an old trunk or chest—or even in some old coin collection that has not been checked for many years.

An Involuntary Gift

In 1864, as the Civil War reached its peak and the Confederacy was at a low ebb, the Southern States made arrangements with S. Straker & Son of London, England, well-known engravers, to produce plates with new designs for the reverses of the Confederacy's paper money. These were made by a then-new process called "Chemiglyphic," developed in Copenhagen in 1843.

The finished plates were shipped to the South, but never reached their destination because of the Union blockade. The ship was seized and its cargo confiscated.

Eventually, the seized material was sold at auction and the engraved plates were purchased for old metal. Later they were rescued by an interested collector.

Over the years, the plates found their way into various collections and were highly prized. Although they had never been used to produce currency, they were of great numismatic and historical value.

Fortunate enough to have one of these plates in my collection, I hit upon a novel idea for using it on my stationery. After discussing the proposed letterhead with a few friends who thought it an excellent idea, I called in a local printer and told him what I had in mind. He said the job could be done without difficulty, and that the printing would be done promptly.

A few days later, I received a call from a young man who worked for the printer. He told me that he had gone to the Secret Service to show them the plate and to find out if it was legal to use it on my stationery. They seized the plate and gave him a receipt and said that they would get in touch with me.

I then heard from the Secret Service authorities that the U.S. Attorney had ruled that under Section 275 of the U. S. Criminal Code USCA Title 18, that it was illegal for me to have that plate and it was permanently confiscated.

In spite of articles appearing in all the coin and stamp publications, letters from coin groups and collectors, as well as attorneys who worked on the matter, it was impossible to recover my property.

It seemed ridiculous to me, particularly in view of the fact that the plate had never been used—even as Confederate Currency— and could not be considered legal tender under any circumstances anywhere in the world.

From time to time I have been asked by the Department of Numismatics at the Smithsonian Institute for items from my collection to be given as gifts to augment material in the Museum. I was, however, never in a position to make a substantial donation to the Smithsonian.

When I visited the new Museum of History and Technology of the Smithsonian Institute recently, in one of their wonderful displays I saw a few of the Chemitype plates—including one of the same denomination as that which had previously been in my own collection. I wonder if I finally have made a gift to the Smithsonian. If so, it pleases me to know that I made a worthwhile donation and that the plate is in good hands.

A Lottery Ticket Lost and Found

Many articles and columns in the newspapers and magazines are devoted to arguing the subject of lotteries, pro and con. The state of New Hampshire has a successful lottery, and there is no doubt that other states will follow suit.

Many people are under the impression that this method of raising funds is new to the United States, thinking of national or state lotteries in connection with Cuba, Mexico, South and Central America, and certain European countries. But lotteries were an important source of revenue in the early days of this country, and were used to raise funds for every conceivable purpose.

Money for building churches, roads, canals, and universities has been raised through lotteries. Lottery tickets bearing many famous signatures—including those of George Washington and John Hancock—are known.

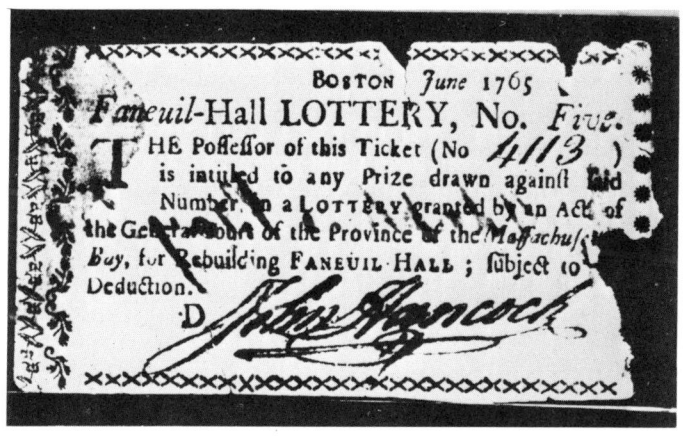

Early Lottery Ticket
This ticket was issued for the rebuilding of Faneuil Hall, Boston, Massachusetts, and is signed by John Hancock.

Faneuil Hall, the "Cradle of Liberty" in Boston, was once rebuilt with funds raised through The Faneuil Hall Lottery of June, 1765, held in Boston. This lottery was granted by An Act of the General Court of the Province of Massachusetts Bay for the rebuilding of Faneuil Hall, and signed by John Hancock, in the same bold handwriting for which he enjoys enduring fame.

One of these lottery tickets was in the stock of a Boston coin dealer who shipped it by insured mail to a collector in Athens, Georgia. This collector's item was never delivered to the addressee and was eventually presumed to have been lost or stolen from the mails.

A photo of this rare item was sent to the numismatic newspaper, Coin World, which published it immediately. Within a few days, a well-known coin dealer in Atlanta, having seen the article and having just purchased the ticket, got in touch with the coin company and the post office authorities.

As a result of the Atlanta dealer's honesy, the Faneuil Hall lottery ticket was returned and the postal inspectors were able to obtain a description of the mail thief.

Each year a bill to permit lotteries again in Massachusettes is introduced before the State Legislature. If this should pass after two hundred years, the lottery funds will, no doubt, again be used for the same purpose, the rebuilding of Faneuil Hall.

Advertising Counterstamps

Until the year 1857, Spanish silver coins were legal tender in the United States and circulated freely. This is why many old lots of coins discovered tucked away in attics and other hiding places, or dug up by farmers and excavators, contain some of these early Spanish and Spanish Colonial pieces.

One of the most interesting uses of these coins was in advertising. Everyone from professional men to saloon keepers would imprint their slogans or addresses on these coins which, being legal tender, circulated freely. Even the famous Woods Minstrels listed their name and address—144 Broadway—on these coins which were sometimes used as admission tickets.

Another group using this kind of advertising was Kunkel's Opera Troupe, organized by George J. Kunkel, one of the first delineators of Negro minstrels in the United States. During his theatrical career, Kunkel was identified with three historic theaters in Baltimore. The infamous John Wilkes Booth was a member of his company at one time, as was the world famous performer, Joe Jefferson.

Several dentists took advantage of this form of advertising and counterstamped coins, "Consult Dr. Darby, Boston," and "Dr. Kimball, Dentist, Boston."

Other coin advertisers included hotels, druggists, saloons, coffee rooms, "segar" stores, magicians, ventriloquists, and brokers.

That the need for hair tonic was as great then as it is today is indicated by such counterstamps as, "Good for a bottle of Pierce's Rosetta Hair Tonic," and "Use Miller's Hair Invigorator."

One unusual item read "R. Flanagan's Punch, 112 N. 6th St.," and shows a punch bowl in the center; another advertises "C. M. Berry Saloon, N. W. C. 5th and Chestnut, Phila."

New pieces of this sort constantly come to hand offering interesting sidelights on the advertising and the economics of the period.

A King of Tokens

What I call a king among tokens is a very large item five inches in diameter and made from lava from Mt. Vesuvius!

The obverse shows Vesuvius in eruption, with the words, "Vesuvius and Millet," at the bottom. The reverse has the legend, "Ward and Howell, 1880, Rochester, New York."

Counterstamp of Spanish 2 Reale Piece
These pieces were current until 1857 and were used to advertise Lanagan's Punch.

Despite correspondence with museums, historical societies, researchers, and collectors, no trace of Ward and Howell can be found.

The edges on this rare piece are rather crude. The lava spilling over the edge of the mold gave the item a very unusual appearance. Tokens are known in many metals and sizes, but I consider this one of the most extraordinary of all.

Odd and Curious Money

Shells, Teeth, Combs, and Hair—East Africa has used a great deal of odd and curious money for barter. Cowrie shell strings, for example, were used by the slave traders to exchange for ivory. Hippo tooth money was also used. For centuries these ivory teeth were an accepted medium of exchange in the Lake Victoria region.

Comb money was used by some tribes in barter for corn meal. These hand-carved combs were made from local wood and designed especially for use in curly hair.

Among the most interesting items are the elephant—and giraffe-hair tokens—bracelets made from the tail hair of elephants and giraffes. These were used mainly by women to purchase medical treatment from the witch doctors. These bracelets were adjustable and tied with special fertility-conferring knots.

Snuff, tobacco, and salt were other frequently used barter materials, packed in small banana-leaf packets, like sausages on a string.

Cloth and Leather Money

During the inflationary period that followed the end of World War I, Germany used every conceivable kind of material for money, including silk, linen, velvet, leather, and wood.

The sheep leather money of Possneck (500,000 marks) and the kid leather money of Osterwieck (1 gold mark), are very scarce.

All of the pieces are beautifully done. Some have satirical pictures, mining scenes, etc. In some cases the edges of the linen money have a wide, white, lace border. Some of the silk money is beautifully embroidered with vibrant and striking colors.

Even though some of the denominations are of high value, because of the tremendous inflation at the time of issue, they did not buy very much.

These pieces make a beautiful display and collections of them have won many prizes at coin shows.

Wooden Money

Hadersfeld, Austria issued wooden money at the end of World War I and in the early 1930's some U.S. firms started using wooden nickels and dimes as depression scrip.

Maundy Money

Maundy money is distributed by the king or queen of England each year in a traditional ceremony that dates back to the 13th century. The original ceremony called for the reigning monarch to distribute gifts of money and clothing to beggars and paupers. Part of the original ceremony was the washing of a beggar's feet by the king or queen, which was considered an act of

German Inflationary Paper Money of 1920's called Notgeld.

humility, as Christ had washed the feet of his disciples. This foot washing was discontinued during the reign of Elizabeth I, as it was considered beneath the dignity of the reigning monarch.

The coin ceremony still takes place on Maundy Thursday and usually is held at Westminster Abbey, with the king or queen distributing the royal Maundy money among the elderly and infirm.

These Maundy coins—never distributed in large numbers—have always been popular with collectors in England. They now have a universal appeal, but only a few dealers have any worthwhile stocks of them.

Issues of even the past few years sell for $65 per set and the 1965 issue has been offered at $75, while the 1953 Coronation date is very rare and sells for $225.

$10,000 *Certificates*

If U.S. Treasury Certificates in unbelievably large denominations, such as $10,000, should blow into your yard, don't start counting your wealth or planning your retirement.

These certificates were once used as a medium of exchange between the Treasury Department and financial institutions. When their use was discontinued, they were stored in the old U.S. Post office building. In 1935, a disastrous fire broke out in the building and firemen found it necessary to dump load after load of these worthless certificates out the windows. Onlookers and curiosity seekers quickly rounded up these appealing souvenirs.

From time to time since the fire a certificate or two has turned up, but the Treasury Department officials tell all of the disappointed and enthusiastic owners this sad story—that the certificate is worthless, that it is illegal contraband, that the notes may not even be held as souvenirs. Although they would make a nice addition to any paper money collection, the notes are then seized. Uninformed optimists holding any of these certificates and making even modest plans to retire on them have a big disappointment in store.

Philippine Guerilla Currency

Among the unusual series of paper money is the emergency money of the Philippine Islands during World War II.

Many of these pieces were brought back by the G.I.'s as souvenirs, but except for one large horde that came to light in recent years, all are considered scarce or rare, particularly if in good condition. The months of circulation in the mountains and in the rugged unoccupied sections of the country caused the notes to be short-lived. These notes were not a speculative issue, but were to be redeemed by the government at a price that would make them more valuable as cash than as a curiosity.

This was good money during the Japanese occupation in contrast to the invasion money the Japanese brought with them which flooded the Island. In the area policed by the Resistance Movement, these notes served as a medium of exchange, although they naturally were of no use in the occupied sections. Anyone found with them ran the risk of torture or execution.

From December 8, 1941 to June 30, 1946, there were twenty-nine Emergency Boards or Committees in operation in different parts of the Island. In all of the provinces, the Boards were identical in function, but the facilities and shortage of paper was such that there are many minor varieties of the paper issued.

These notes were a tremendous morale booster to civilians, government officials, and guerillas alike. They were regarded as tangible proof that freedom would someday be restored. To the masses they were more valuable than the Japanese notes and the guerillas took advantage of this value in purchasing food, clothing, and supplies. It was largely for this reason that the Japanese tortured or beheaded anyone caught with the notes, for they fully realized that these notes were a symbol of resistance.

A great many notes were never returned for redemption because the poor and fragile quality of the paper and the wear and tear of circulation in the mountain hideouts made many pieces unrecognizable for redemption purposes. In some cases, entire villages retired to the mountains and these notes became their medium of exchange.

Very few places in the Philippines have printing or lithography shops, so notes were printed from woodcuts, or mimeographed, and in some cases, even typewritten.

As there was a shortage of ink, often lampblack mixed with some fluid was used. Every possible type of paper was utilized—from toilet paper and manila wrapping paper to the lined paper of Government account books.

This is one of the few series of notes that was subject to very little counterfeiting. The Moros did try to counterfeit some of the higher denominations, but their imitations were too crude to deceive anyone, except the most illiterate peasant.

A few commanders in the field issued their own notes, but not all of these were recognized, and only a few received special authority from Washington or from Australia for redemption.

After the United States drove out the Japanese, legislation was passed for the redemption of all guerilla and emergency issues during the following year and for invalidating all those not registered within a fixed period.

One of the finest collections was assembled by the late Allan Forbes of Boston, Chairman of the Board of the State St. Trust Company, and one of the country's best known collectors. He presented his collection to the Massachusetts Historical Society and the collection is now in their archives.

VII

■

The Interesting World of the Exonumist

History repeats itself in the large increase of Exonumia enthusiasts collecting tokens, medals, and other affiliated material; the formation of a national Token and Medal Society, which has grown by leaps and bounds; and the publication of many new pamphlets and books in this field.

One hundred years ago, similar enthusiasm prevailed and almost all numismatic books and auction catalogs contained such material as tokens, medals, and political items. Records were kept of the prices realized at auctions and for the first time listings were made. These have proved invaluable to students and numismatists in compiling and recording factual information.

In the 1860's, Washington coins, medals, and tokens were

Lincoln Medal issued in 1909 on occasion of the Centennial of his birth.

in demand. Among the prices realized were the following: Liverpool half-pennies, several varieties of ships, $4.35; Washington Benevolent Society, 1808, silver, $4.00; Washington Temperance Medal, $1.50; George Washington, with reverse, Washington on horseback silver, $14.50; Head of Washington, reverse Wright & Bale, die cutters, etc. $5.00; The rare Wolf, Clark & Spies Card, $4.00.

Other pieces brought amounts from 18¢ to $64.00 for a

Washington half-dollar struck in copper, commonly called "The Large Eagle Cent of 1792," in splendid Proof condition.

Presidential and election medals and medalets were very popular and some of the pieces and the prices realized were: Andrew Jackson, reverse, THE UNION MUST AND SHALL BE PRESERVED, THE BANK MUST PERISH, $2.00; William Henry Harrison, reverse, BUNKER HILL MONUMENT, HARRISON JUBILEE, BUNKER HILL, SEPTEMBER 10, 1840, White metal, $1.50; Martin Van Buren, reverse TEMPLE OF LIBERTY, DEMOCRACY AND OUR COUNTRY, white metal, $1.25; Henry Clay, reverse YOUNG MENS' CONVENTION, BALTIMORE, 1844, white medal, $1.75.

The auctions also offered political items pertaining to Cass, Polk, Taylor, Fillmore, Scott, Pierce, Buchanan, and Fremont. These pieces brought from 10¢ to $2.50 each, depending on their rarity. Some of the political tokens brought from 3¢ for the common varieties to $2.50 for The Glorious Whig Victory token of 1835.

A series in which there has been recently revived interest is the temperance tokens and medalets. These pieces were popular in the 1880's and brought prices ranging from 25¢ to $1.50 each. Today the same pieces bring from $1.00 to $10.00.

Other items collected were California counters, merchants tokens, Sage & Lovett pieces, Canadian tokens, and communion tokens. Each specialist devoted himself to his particular taste. Medals were extremely popular, with those pertaining to early America most eagerly sought after.

When one thinks of the value of a day's wage a hundred years ago, it can be seen that the prices were high for the period. Items like Massachusetts Pine Tree and Oak Tree silvers, in nice condition, brought $4 to $5 each, and a 1793 half-cent, $4. "Oddball" material was obviously in demand and bringing excellent prices.

There have been other periods in numismatic history when

Political Token used during the Presidential Campaign of 1840

the unusual material took its rightful place again for a number of years, and the current revival of interest in this kind of collecting suggests there will be thousands of new collectors in the future.

Many famous exonumists are now writing monographs and doing other specialized work that will be of help to many generations of collectors. This field has unlimited possibilities for the real numismatist who does not want to be limited in the scope of his interests and is always looking for the rainbow around the corner.

Encased Postage Stamps

During the Civil War there was a great shortage of small change, not unlike that experienced in 1965.

In 1862 John Gault, a Boston merchant, patented an item consisting of a circular metal holder with a mica front in which postage stamps of various denominations were placed. The reverse of the holder carried an advertisement of the firm issuing the stamps. Denominations were from 1¢ to 90¢.

Unfortunately, the cost of encasing the stamps and manufacturing the holders proved prohibitive and Gault's Encased Stamps never achieved wide circulation.

The higher denominations are quite rare and the 90¢ stamp is seldom offered.

The shortage of hard money became so acute that citizens used regular stamps as substitutes for nickels, dimes, and quarters. This did not work out, however, as the stamps often became stuck together, torn or wrinkled until they could not even be used for postage on a letter.

Many people with quantities of mutilated and stuck-together stamps took them to the post office to exchange for new stamps. At first, postmasters would refuse to exchange such items since the government claimed that the stamps were sold for use on letters and not to be used as money.

Encased Postage Stamp used during the Coin Shortage of the Civil War.

Eventually, after a number of conferences, it was agreed to allow old stamps to be exchanged for new ones.

During this period, the Treasurer of the United States conceived the idea of Postage Currency, which was the term applied to small notes in denominations of 3¢ to 50¢. The first issues had pictures of current postage on them.

The first issue consisted of 5¢, 10¢, 25¢, and 50¢ denominations.

The 5¢ Jefferson and 10¢ Washington postage stamps were used in the designs, since these items were well known to the general public.

The 5¢ Note used a single 5¢ stamp design, while the 25¢ notes had five 5¢ stamps. The 10¢ note had one 10¢ stamp copy and the 50¢ note was engraved with five 10¢ stamps.

These notes were legitimate legal tender. Postage and fractional currency were used from 1862 to 1876. It is estimated that some 1,800,000 notes remain unredeemed or undestroyed.

There was a great deal of counterfeiting of these pieces, but most of the fakes were crude and easily detected.

Some of the fractional currency pieces have autographed signatures. These are all scarce and highly desirable.

Buck Island

Buck Island is a tiny land mass in the Caribbean waters of the British Virgin Islands.

Coins used on the island are suitably called "One Buck" and "Half-a-Buck." These, as a medium of exchange for the purchase of goods and services, carry the same value as U.S. dollars and half-dollars.

The one buck coin is approximately the size of a U.S. silver dollar, the half buck is similar in size and weight to an American fifty cent piece.

Curio seekers and collectors have been known to charter boats for as much as $125 a day to travel from the U.S. island of St. Thomas to Buck Island, 28 miles to the east, in order to obtain these unusual and little-known coins.

These attractive coins show the head of a typical island buck or goat—similar to the African antelope—with the legend, ONE BUCK. The reverse shows a relief of the island and its precise geographic location in navigational terms, 18°25'45"N-64°33'30" W and the legend BUCK ISLAND B.V.I.

These pieces have created a great deal of interest in the numismatic world and are quite popular.

Embossed Cards of the 1860's

Embossed cards are advertising novelties made mostly in the 1860's, usually the size of a silver dollar, and are fashioned of heavy cardboard.

They usually have the head of Liberty, with the date underneath on the obverse; the reverse will have the name of a product, with an eagle or other trademark and are mostly gilded to resemble a $20 gold piece.

Many of these items have been destroyed over the years and it is difficult to find them in nice condition. In the 1860's many

Embossed Card of 1868

of the country's leading firms used this form of advertising and many exonumist and token collectors are eagerly seeking them.

Jenny Lind is only one of the famous beauties whose pictures appear on these cards. There are some known of George Washington, who appears on the obverse, and these are quite rare.

Condition is very important as many of the cards are found badly stained, torn, and mutilated. In nice condition these items are estimated to be worth $10 to $35 each.

Counterstamps

Counterstamped or countermarked coins hold a fascination for many numismatists.

The E.B. stamped on a 1799 dollar is the mark of Ephraim Brasher, famous in numismatics for the Ephraim Brasher doubloon, one of the world's rarest coins.

One of the rarest Hawaiian items is the counterstamp on a U.S. half-dollar of 1872 of the Thomas Hobron Hawaiian token. It is believed Unique and was originally in the collection of the author.

Str. Jewel, struck on an 1853 quarter, refers to the *Steamer Jewel,* which was a coastwise craft running from Portland, Maine, to Gardiner and also to Nova Scotia about 1900.

Some U.S. copper and silver coins are known with various Masonic counterstamps. In some cases the reverse and obverse have been shaved and then engraved for use as Royal Arch Chapter pennies.

Among the political tokens is an American Large Cent counterstamped, VOTE THE LAND FREE. These were circulated during the presidential election of 1848. Part of the platform of the Free Soil Party was, "Whereas we have assembled in convention as a union of free men for the sake of freedom, forgetting all past political differences, in common resolve to maintain the rights of all free labor against the aggression of a

Unusual Group of Counterstamped Coins

slave power and to secure free soil for a free people." The slogan in this campaign was, "Free Soil, Free Speech, and Free Men."

The countermarked and cut coins of the West Indies are among the most glamorous of this series. To date, many have not been attributed, even though a great many scholars have worked in this field for years.

Authority for the use of many of the counterstamps is to be found in the laws and ordinances of different islands. Some of the stamps were used within the Napoleonic War period when the flags of several of the islands changed hands according to the fortunes of war. Among these counterstamps are included a rose with five petals, used in Curacao during the English occupation, 1807-15.

Cuba used a "key" counterstamp. Dominica had a circular

piece cut from the center of Spanish Pillar dollars and this section was stamped with a script "D" enclosing a star within a circle of rays. Some of the dollars have been found stamped with "16" and a crown above it. Silver, copper, and gold coins of the West Indies have been countermarked. An ordinance was passed in Martinique in 1805 authorizing the countermarking of gold half-joes with a stamp having the figures "20" or "22" over a small eagle, these coins to have a value of 20 or 22 livres.

During the 18th century there was a shortage of change and silver in England, because no silver larger than a four-pence had been coined for a number of years.

The English government had in its vault a huge number of Spanish dollars taken from various captured vessels. Because of the tremendous demand for change, the government decided to place the Spanish Pillar dollars on the market.

In order to give official sanction for this experiment, the English king's head was stamped on the head of the Spanish king. This was the stamp used at Goldsmith's Hall for marking silver plate.

On March 6, 1797, a public notice appeared that the bank would supply these coins and because they were in such demand, there was a great rush for this counterstamped money. Over 2,325,000 pieces were issued.

As soon as the dollars were issued by the bank, some cunning counterfeiters set to work and issued counterfeit impressions of the King's head and stamped Spanish dollars to their own advantage.

Because of this, the Bank of England called in the dollars and issued a notice that they would no longer be redeemable after October 31, 1797.

My good friend Major Sheldon S. Carroll, Curator of the Numismatic Museum of the Bank of Canada, told me an interesting story concerning the identification of counterstamps on a group of coins.

Eight coins that were part of an old estate were found with the following counterstamped letters and figures: PW ESQ AE 59; AW AE 59; TW; PW J; CCW; CHW; AB.

The initial "W" appeared on all of the coins and the "PW" was a well known monogram to anyone in the Ottawa area, being that of Philomen Wright, famous as the founder of the city of Ottawa in 1802. Wright had moved from Massachusetts to the Ottawa section of Canada with his family and a sizable group of forty or fifty friends, who thought to prosper in the new territory.

His savings amounted to $40,000, a considerable sum in 1802. After checking various locations for suitability, Wright built a tannery, a bakery, and several other buildings that formed the nucleus of his colony.

The industrious settlement prospered and Wright, who soon became known as "The King of Ottawa," built the first steamboat on the Ottawa River.

Major Carroll, a great researcher and student of numismatics, tried to unravel the meanings of the other initials on the various coins. By checking many museums and libraries, he found information about Wright, who with his wife, Abigail, raised a family of six children, including Philomen Jr., Christopher Columbus, Ruggles, Tiberius, Christina and Abigail.

In his research, Major Carroll discovered that Philomen Wright signed his name, P. WRIGHT, ESQ.

The Major's final important source of information was the original will of Abigail Wright with the following clause for Philomen Jr.: "I wish him to have the singular dollar which his father left to me." Further on in the will she mentioned that she wished Tiberius to have the coin known as Pistareen.

The coins consisted of a Spanish dollar, a U.S. half-dollar dated 1805, and six Spanish 2 reales. All of these, being current coins during the early period, could certainly could have been used by the early settlers.

The AE was construed by Major Carroll to have been used in place of the Latin word *aetatia* meaning "aged." Combined with previous researches this yielded the following identifications: PW ESQ AE 50 (Philomen Wright, Esq. Aged 50); AW AE 50 (Abigail Wright, aged 50); TW (Tiberius Wright); PWJ (Philomen Wright Jr.); CCW (Christopher Columbus Wright; RW (Ruggles Wright); CHW (Christina H. Wright, middle name probably Hanna which was a popular name in the Wright family); AB (Abigail Brigham formerly Abigail Wright Jr. who married Thomas Brigham).

The dates of the eight coins were as follows: 1721, 172(?), 172(?), 172(?), 1737, 1759, 1776, 1804, 1817.

Naturally these keepsakes would have been treasured by the various members of the family and held for many years. There remains the mystery of how the coins found their way into the one estate after having been distributed and probably carried to all parts of the world.

Political Items

One of the most enthusiastic specialists in numismatics is the collector of political items. In recent years this series has come to the foreground and many new collectors have found it an exciting sidelight to the more usual forms of collecting.

A dynamic and active group has formed a national organization called The American Political Collectors Club, which has a growing membership and now issues a quarterly bulletin.

During Presidential election years, many exhibits are shown and many new collections are originated with the current year's Presidential material.

The usual political information can be found in any American history book, but the student of this series will know, for instance, that there are three present day minor parties—the Theocratic Party, whose 1964 candidates included Bishop Homer Tomlinson and W. R. Rogers for president and vice-

Political Token of the Prohibition Party Candidates of 1964.

president; the Socialist Workers Party which was the first U.S. party to have a Negro candidate for president; and the Prohibition Party with E. Harold Munn, Sr., and Mark R. Shaw of Massachusetts candidates for president and vice-president in 1964.

Political collectors will know that The Half Breeds were a liberal wing of the Republican Party opposed to the third term of Ulysses S. Grant between 1876 and 84 and finally supporting Garfield in 1880; that, the Mugwumps were independent members of the Republican Party, who were against Blaine in 1884 and supported Cleveland, the Democratic candidate, who was often referred to as Mug and Wump, depending on which party was discussing him. The Scalawags were the white Southerners who supported the reconstruction policies of the Radical Republicans of the South after the Civil War.

Sought by political collectors are items ranging from the inaugural buttons worn by dignitaries at George Washington's inaugural, to present-day Goldwater, Johnson, Rockefeller, and Lodge buttons.

Many of the rarest and scarcest pieces are those pertaining to the candidates who lost in elections. Usually, not many pieces were struck, and after a candidate's defeat, the items would normally be destroyed.

Among items collected are newspapers, ballots, ribbons, tokens, medals, pins, badges—anythinng mentioning the candidates or their campaign slogans.

George Washington Inaugural Button

The most famous series of political items are the Bryan pieces. While this famous American never attained the Presidency, he was a candidate many times and there are many political items connected with his various campaigns. Among the best known are the Bryan dollars, struck by such famous silversmiths as Tiffany and Gorham. Many of the Bryan pieces bear the slogan, "16 to 1," referring to the ratio of silver to gold and one of the best-known resolutions of his platform.

One of the most famous collections formed in this field was that of J. Doyle DeWitt of Hartford, Connecticut. This collection has been exhibited to the public a number of times. His excellent book is considered the bible of political token collecting.

Indian Peace Medals

Indian medals were highly prized by the tribal chiefs and were given to those who were friendly or who had performed some important service for the French, British, or Americans, who issued these medals in North America in the 1700's and 1800's.

The Indian medals, in most cases, were struck in silver and were holed, having a leather thong to allow the medal to be worn as a pendant.

When prominent statesmen or governors came to the Colonies, they would bring a number of the Indian medals with them. On the British medals, the King was usually pictured on the obverse; the reverse having the royal arms. One extremely rare early piece is dated 1714, and has a bust of George I in armor on the obverse; the reverse shows an Indian drawing a bow on a deer; the sun is above; to the right are three stars, and to the left, one. One of these medals was found in 1814 at an Indian burial place in Wilkes Barre, Pennsylvania, by Pennsylvania Supreme Court Chief Justice Gibson and two companions. One in a very good state of preservation recently came to light in a Boston suburb.

Anther unusual Indian medal, dated 1764, shows a landscape on the reverse. In the foreground is a military officer, to the right an Indian seated on a rustic chair by the bank of a river. Also, a house on a rocky point where the river flows into the ocean where there are three ships under full sail. The Indian holds a pipe in his left hand and his right hand grasps the officer's hand. The obverse has a portrait of George III, bust facing right, with the Ribbon of the Garter.

When Indians came to visit the white settlements, in some localities, the chief was required to wear a badge to make known who was responsible for the conduct of the Indians should there be pilfering, looting, or other damage. The early medals designed for this purpose were hand-engraved and were actually badges. Several pieces are known for the Pamunkeys, a tribe of Indians in Virginia. On the obverse of some of these medals a tobacco plant is engraved—tobacco being the principal commodity of colonial Virginia.

A medal of special interest to Canadians is one issued in 1760. The obverse shows a view of a fortified town with five steeples and five bastions. A river shows in front. On the right is a fort with a flag flying over it. The hand-engraved reverse has the following inscription: TEKAHON WAGHSE ONONDAGOS. Below, in three lines: TAKEN FROM AN INDIAN CHIEF IN AMERICAN WAR 1761. Another piece of the same type is known, with the inscription: MADOGHK, MOHICKANS. These can be classed as war medals presented to the members of the tribes who assisted in the capture of Montreal in 1760.

In dealing with the Indians, the Americans used large silver peace medals which were presented to the chiefs. These usually had a bust of the president on the obverse, while the reverse showed hands clasped in friendship. These pieces are highly sought after by both collectors and museums and there is a particular demand for those issued with the portrait of Abraham

Lincoln.

The obverse of a French medal issued in 1693 has a bust of the King of France, the reverse has a bust of the Dauphin, a bust of the Duke D'Anjou, or a bust of the Duke DeBerry. All of the above are in profile, with flowing hair. Although this medal was not originally struck for presentation purposes, it eventually was used for presentation to the Indian chiefs.

Another unusual French Indian medal shows two warriors standing with hands clasped. One, representing France, is wearing a Roman tunic and holds a spear in his left hand. The other, representing France's Indian allies, also holds a spear in his left hand. Interestingly, this medal has been found with the name of King Louis XV removed, and George III engraved in its place. Possibly the English needing a presentation piece in a hurry and not having any of their own available, decided that "necessity was the mother of invention." Since we know that this was done once, it is reasonable to assume that it might have been done on several other occasions.

There are a few early and interesting religious Indian medals of the 1680's. One of these Catholic medals was originally struck for the Mexican Indians. Another has a bust of a female saint on the obverse, with the legend, SANTA ROSA DE LIMA ORD. RON. The reverse has a bust of St. Paul with arms crossed holding a crucifix. This particular piece was discovered at the site of an Indian village as Scipioville, in Cayuga County, New York, where a mission, begun in 1656, continued for approximately thirty years. Research has shown that the village of Scipioville probably consisted of captive Hurons.

Other religious medals and crosses have been excavated from the same area, but only the St. Paul medal seems to have been struck for Peru.

A Spanish medal is known with the obverse in Spanish, translated, "Charles III, King of Spain and the Indies," with a bust of the king. The reverse has the legend FOR MERIT, within a wreath of cactus. This medal seems as if it might have been used for some kind of award though it was discovered at Prairie du Schien about 1864 and was supposed to have been given by the Spanish Governor to Huisconsin, a Matisse chief of the Sauks and Foxes.

Many of these medals are called peace medals for they allude to keeping the peace between red man and white. On many occasions, presentations were made at special ceremonies with entire villages, soldiers, and settlers participating. Feasting and rejoicing would be followed by smoking the peace pipe and the formal presentation of the medal.

These medals became one of the chief's valued possessions. They were handed down from generation to generation. Some of those that I have handled show a great deal of wear. They were obviously used and worn for many important occasions.

An enterprising business firm in the east turned out a large number of copies of the American-type medals. These were sold to traders for use in dealings with the Indians. This was highly profitable to the traders, since the Indians were quite anxious to obtain medals that only chiefs had previously possessed.

In the medals still being struck at the U.S. Mint today, many of the presidential medals incorporate on the reverse the hands clasped in friendship, tomahawk, etc.

The Box Dollar or Taler

Fantastically simple and yet most ingenious was the use to which old European dollar-size coins or trade dollars were put. The value of their content was much greater than the face value of the coins themselves.

By removing the center of the coin in such a way that the piece still looked as it had before the work was done, it was possible to insert various objects into the hollow. The coin actually was a small hollow box—hence the term "box dollar." Except for weight, it was impossible to tell the difference between these and any such coins in regular circulation, so clever was the skillful workmanship.

Smuggling opium from the Orient and the transmitting of top secret messages were only two of the uses attributed to these dollars. They were also used in romantic intrigues and when opened, some were found to contain a lock of hair or a photo of a loved one. It is believed that some of the American trade dollars were prepared and sold as souvenirs at the Columbian Exposition in Chicago in 1893.

There is usually a secret hinge hidden at the bottom of the coin that opens immediately when pressure is applied.

One of the most unusual of the early European box talers is Augsburg, Ferdinand II, The Holy Roman Emperor. The obverse of this beautiful coin has a bust of the Emperor. The reverse has a view of the city and a pineapple. Inside of some of these pieces are perfect sets of colored mica pictures. There is one on display at the Smithsonian Institute with colored pictures inside-Nuremberg, by W.P. Werner, 1730.

Who knows but that perhaps some contemporary coin is being used for a similar purpose?

The $100 Token

The token which I believe has the largest denomination is the $100 token of Ormsby & Co. Dated 1849, with the figures "100" and the reverse legend, "J.S.O." this token also has "$100 dolls." on the obverse, with twelve slightly irregular stars bordering the edge.

One hundred dollars was a fabulous sum in 1848, except in the California gold camps, where, with new strikes making miners wealthy overnight, this denomination probably was useful. Prices at the camps were so inflated that the price of a night's lodging or a bath was more than a man could make for a full week's work in the East.

J.S. Ormsby & Co., of Sacramento, California operated both an assay office and mint. The firm included some prominent

Californians, among whom was Dr. Ormsby himself, a member of the California legislature. The company also issued $5 and $10 Territorial gold, both of which are extremely rare. Theirs is the only token that has ever been found in the $100 denomination. My own theory is that this piece was given as a receipt for a hundred dollars worth of gold dust until Ormsby could mint coins for the owner of the token, who would redeem the token for the gold pieces when they were ready.

J. S. Ormsby $100 Token

VIII

Colonial Hog Money, Pine Trees, and Bungtown Coppers

Early U.S. Colonial Coins

U.S. Colonial coins from the years 1612 to 1795 bring to mind some of the most fascinating aspects of American history.

The earliest American coinage was minted in 1612 at Sommers Island—now called Bermuda. These pieces were named "Hog Money" in commemoration of the abundance of hogs on the island when the colonists landed.

In 1631, Massachusetts used corn as legal tender at market prices. In 1634, musket bullets passed current for a farthing apiece.

The first U.S. Colonial coinage made its appearance in Massachusetts in 1652 after the mint was established at Boston and coins with values of 3 pence, 6 pence, and 12 pence were

Pine Tree Six Pence of 1652

struck. These coins were to be of the finest of new sterling English money. They were stamped "N.E." on one side and with the value on the reverse. Such simplicity of design left the coins exposed to easy washing and clipping.

To remedy this situation, it was decreed that the shillings and the smaller pieces would have a double ring on either side, with the inscription "Massachusetts" and a tree in the center of the obverse and the date on the reverse.

In 1662, the 2 pence coin was added to this series.

These coins are known as the Pine Tree, Oak Tree, and Willow Tree shillings, 6 pence and 3 pence. They are among the most sought U.S. Colonial pieces.

Although the Massachuesetts Mint existed for approximately thirty-four years, all of the coins issued there are dated either 1652 or 1662. Undoubtedly the same dies were used throughout the life of the mint.

During the reign of William and Mary, England struck copper coins for New England and Carolina. These have an elephant on the obverse, and "God Preserve New England

New England Numismatic Association Medal

1694," or "God preserve Carolina," "The Lord's Proprietors 1694" on the reverse.

As early as 1661, an Act was passed by the Assembly of Maryland to set up a mint within the Province, but shillings, 6 pence, 4 pence, and groats of silver were made in England under the direction of Lord Baltimore.

U.S. State Coinage

In Vermont, a mint was established by legislative authority in 1785 and copper cents were issued. The obverse has a sun rising from behind hills, with a plow in the foreground, and the legend, "Vermontensium Res Publica 1786." The reverse shows a radiated eye surrounded by thirteen stars and the legend, "Quarta Decima Stella."

The cents of 1788 have a head with the legend, "Vermon Auctori" on the obverse; and a woman seated, the lettering, "Inde et Lib," and the date on the reverse. There are many other varieties in this series.

Connecticut followed the example of Vermont and in the same year, 1785, authorized the establishment of a mint at New Haven. From 1785 to 1788, many varieties of Connecticut cents were issued.

Massachusetts had state coinage in 1787 and 1788; New Jersey and New York,, from 1786 to 1788.

Massachusetts Colonial Half Cent of 1787

French Crown of the 1730's

Coins were minted for the French Colonies in 1721 and 1722 and again in 1767.

There are a number of different varieties of the Continental dollar struck in 1776. These even include varied spellings of the word "Currency."

Colonial collecting requires much patience and study, but the rewards to the collector are well worth the effort.

Colonial Counterfeiting

We all know that our modern laws are severe for counterfeiting, but in Massachusetts in 1786, a law was passed called AN ACT AGAINST COUNTERFEITING, OR UTTERING COUNTERFEIT COIN—"Be It Enacted by the Senate and House of Representatives in General Court Assembled, and by the Authority of the Same, That if any Person Shall Forge, or Counterfeit any silver or gold money, or coin, the currency of which is or shall be established and regulated by law, or shall forge or counterfeit any silver or gold money, or coin, that is or shall be current in this Commonwealth, he shall be fined, at the discretion of the Court; be set in the pillory for the space of one hour, and then have one of his ears cut off; and from thence be drawn to the gallows, and set thereon with a rope about his neck for the space of one hour, and shall be whipped not exceeding forty stripes, and shall then be sentenced to hard labour for a term of not more than seven years."

You can readily see how harsh and severe a punishment was deemed to fit the crime of counterfeiting. A great deal of the early Colonial currency bears the slogan TO COUNTERFEIT IS DEATH.

The law goes on to cite coloring or gilding of coins to make silver look like gold or altering copper coins to make them resemble gold or silver: "He shall be judged guilty of forging and counterfeiting."

The punishment was just about the same as that for regular

counterfeiting, and was specified in the statute.

Also specified was that informers would receive rewards of twenty-five pounds out of the public treasury "For informing and prosecuting to conviction counterfeiters."

Bungtowns

Aside from a few advanced U.S. Colonial collectors, very few people have heard of the term "Bungtown."

Bungtown is the term applied to the early copper coins circulated in the Colonies through the late 1600's and 1700's.

These coins, though made to look like English half-pennies, have no value designated on them. In most instances, they have a seated figure of Britannia or a Crowned Harp on the reverse.

The obverse, or front of the coin, usually has a portrait or bust of some well-known figure like Shakespeare, or the King of England. In many cases, words have been misspelled and satirical phrases are sometimes used.

Many of these pieces were not well struck and when they went into circulation they looked a good deal like the worn copper that was handled daily.

The Bungtowns have also been called Tory Pennies. While they circulated in all of the colonies, they were particularly well-known in Pennsylvania.

Research continues to be done on this series and some day we will have more complete information about this group of coins.

Paul Revere

Paul Revere's many accomplishments as silversmith, as well as his patriotic activities are familiar to collectors and historians. However, little is known generally about Revere's work in the field of numismatics except by a few advanced collectors who are familiar with his background through personal interest and research.

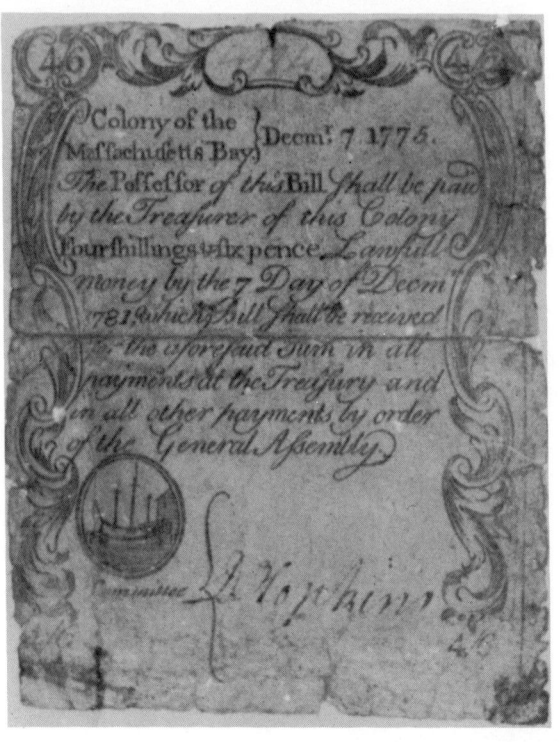

Colonial Note Engraved by Paul Revere, December 7, 1775.

Two unusual Massachusetts coins—both of which are unique—are attributed to Paul Revere. One piece, known as The Massachusetts Pine Tree Copper, has a pine tree on the obverse, with the legend, MASSACHUSSETTS STATE. The reverse has the Goddess of Liberty facing left, seated upon a globe supporting the Staff of Liberty with her left hand and holding the cap extended in her right; at her feet sits a dog.

The other piece, The Massachusetts Janus Head Half-Penny, sometimes called "The Janus Copper," has three heads combined instead of the usual two-faced Janus head. The obverse shows the three heads with the legend, MASSA. 1/2 D. The reverse shows the Goddess of Liberty facing right, resting against a globe. Her right hand supports the staff of Liberty and in her left she holds a cap; a dog is seated at her feet. The legend on the reverse reads, GODDESS LIBERTY 1776.

When the Janus Head was discovered, it was found with some Proof impressions from plates for Continental Paper Currency which had been engraved by Paul Revere. Revere also engraved some Colonial notes, the most famous of which are the Massachusetts Sword in Hand notes. All are extremely rare.

Visitors to Boston may visit the Boston Museum of Fine Arts, where the Paul Revere room houses the largest collection of Revere material known, including many privately-owned pieces on loan for this exhibit.

The Massachusetts Historical Society's collection contains the only known Janus Head and Massachusetts Pine Tree Copper, as well as a genuine 1804 silver dollar and many other rarities.

Continental Currency

The Continental currencies used during the Revolutionary War all have interesting Latin inscriptions. Many of these are unusual and fascinating.

The $2 bill bears the inscription, translated from the Latin, "Affliction and riches." The $3 bill, "The end is in doubt." The $4 bill, "Either death or an honorable life." And the $6 bill, "By persevering."

Also, the $50 bill, "Everlasting," the $60 bill, "The Lord reigneth, let the world rejoice," and the $45 bill, "Thus flourishes the Republic."

The $55 bill, "After the cloud comes the sun," the $65 bill, "Let justice be done," and the $80 bill, "It will flourish forever and ever."

One of the fractional denomination notes uses "Fugio, Mind Your Business," a slogan also made famous on a Colonial coin, the Fugio cent conceived by Benjamin Franklin. Both the coin and the note have a sundial in the center.

The phrase, "Not worth a continental," came from these early notes, for when owners tried to redeem them, they were almost valueless.

It is said that the soldiers in Washington's army, whose boots and shoes were in sad need of repair, stuffed their soles with this Continental money to keep out the bitter cold.

The series of May, 1777, and April 11, 1778, were withdrawn and mostly destroyed; the balance then in circulation was repudiated because of the many counterfeits flooding the Colonies.

Many early Colonial notes have signatures of the signers of the Declaration of Independence and other important figures of the early Revolutionary period.

Revolutionary $8 Note called Continental Currency

IX

■

Numismatics of Canada

The Canadian series are very popular among collectors today. But in the 1930's, there was very little activity in Canadian numismatics. There were no standard catalogs or holders for the Canadian coins and except for rarities, most pieces could be obtained for a little over face value. For instance, the regular price of an 1858 Proof five-cent piece was 50¢ and no one cared that it might be a large or a small date. Uncirculated large cents sold for 5¢ and 10¢ each.

The early Canadian coin collector was both student and avid numismatist. Many of the most important names in the world of numismatics are those of the early Canadian collectors.

When the American Numismatic Association was formed in the 1890's, one of its officers and several of the charter members were Canadians.

In 1950, Major Sheldon Carroll formed a group of collectors into the now internationally known Canadian Numismatic Association, which at the present time has members from coast to coast, maintains an excellent coin publication and sponsors annual national conventions.

American collectors have been interested in all phases of Canadian numismatics and this interest and support has contributed to the fantastic increase in values of Canadian material.

I remember a well-known Canadian dealer bidding at a New England Numismatic Association auction in 1958. He and a few other collectors present pushed many scarce Canadian coins to new record highs. At the time, I thought they were going berserk and would never be able to recoup their investments for some of the pieces brought two and three times catalog value at that auction.

Recently that same dealer sold a portion of his collection for approximately $75,000. He certainly proved himself an astute buyer. Moreover, this lot was bought by another dealer, who in turn would sell the items at a profit!

A great educational surge is taking place in the field of Canadian numismatics. The bi-monthly publication, *Canadian Coin, Stamp and Antique News* and other literature and periodicals are available for novice and advanced collector alike. Reprints of many rare and out of print books have also been a boon to the student.

The Canadian series has many interesting fields in addition to the decimal material. There are communion tokens, for instance, and blacksmith tokens, various medals, and other specialized series which are of interest to the exonumist.

Radio and television stations in Canada have sponsored programs on coin collecting and some newspapers have carried daily quotations on investment material. All this helps stimulate interest in the hobby.

Boer War Canadian Medal 1900

One thing to be remembered is the small mintage of Canadian coins as compared to U.S. issues. Many Canadian issues are of approximately 1,000,000 pieces and—except in the recent years—very few exceed 5,000,000. When one gets into the coinage of Newfoundland, many run as low as 20,000 to 100,000 coins minted. It can easily be seen that with the increase in collectors, such material could be very easily absorbed.

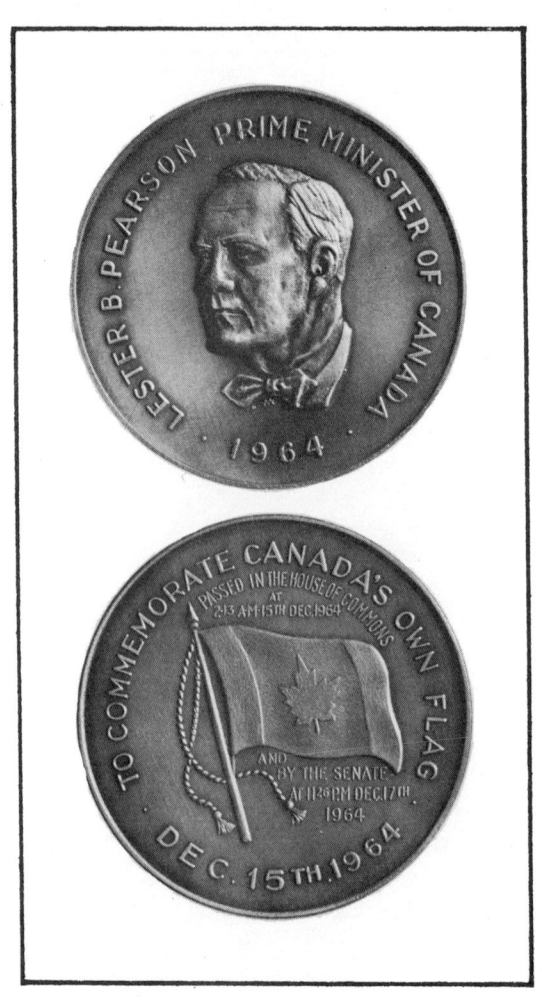

Canadian Prime Minister Medal, 1964

Canadian Paper Money

Paper money collectors, or "rag pickers" as they have sometimes been nicknamed, have long been considered the stepchildren of numismatics. However, as a rule, this type of collector is as serious a numismatist as the coin collector and is always looking for information and eager to better the specimens in his collection.

The Canadian Fractional Notes, called "Shinplasters" were only issued in three years: 1870, 1900, and 1923.

There are several different signatures and varieties. The 1870 series comes with the letter A, with the letter B, and with no letter. The letter A is the scarcest of all the fractional items and is very difficult to obtain in crisp condition.

The Saunders of 1900 is the scarcest of the three signatures found in that year. In 1923, the Hyndman-Saunders signature combination is by far the scarcest. These signatures also come in either red or black.

Most easily obtainable is the 1923 Campbell-Clark and the McCavour-Saunders, which can be purchased for a very nominal sum.

Some collectors try to obtain one of each letter. I have been told that it is still possible to complete the series. It is estimated that approximately 4,000,000 Shinplasters are still outstanding, but obviously many would have disappeared or been destroyed over the years.

One of the most popular series is the regular Canadian notes, including The Province of Canada; Dominion of Canada; Bank of Canada, and the Chartered Notes.

The Province of Canada notes run from the $1 to $500 denomination. They are beautifully engraved and most of them are difficult to obtain in really nice condition. The vignettes picture Canadian history and economics. All of these are dated 1866 and signed by T. D. Harington.

The Dominion of Canada notes were first issued in 1870 in $1, $2, and $50 denominations. The $50 denomination is very rare. These notes also have beautiful vignettes and make fine additions to any collection.

Notes of the well-known 1878 issue—which features the Countess of Dufferin on the $1 bill—are payable in St. John, Halifax, Toronto, and Montreal.

The 1882 issue includes one of Canada's most sought bills—the $4 note with the portrait of the Marquis of Lorne-Courtney. Because of the odd denomination, this note is desired in all conditions.

The $2 1887 issue features the Marquis and Marchioness of Lansdowne-Courtney.

The $1 and $2 denominations in the 1897 issue, and the 1898 $1 issue with the Earl and Countess of Aberdeen, are well designed notes. The 1898 issue has two different signatures.

In 1900 another $4 bill was issued. This note is also popular with collectors.

The 1911 issues, in the large denominations of $500 and $1,000, are extremely rare.

The 1924 issue featured a $5 bill with a portrait of Queen Mary. There are many varieties in the series from 1912 to date which collectors will find listed in detail in the books on Canadian paper money and in catalogs where the notes are priced in the different conditions.

Notes of the chartered banks present a tremendous challenge as there are quite a number and notes have been issued since 1817. New information continues to become available and perhaps a complete listing will someday be possible.

The Bank of Montreal was the first to issue chartered notes. The Bank of Nova Scotia, the Bank of New Brunswick, and others followed. Notes of the Summerside Bank of Prince Edward Island are extremely rare since there are very few notes outstanding, but one of them showed up at a New England convention only a few years ago.

It takes a great deal of patience and effort to assemble a sizable collection of this series and with very few of the early notes available in many cases, an influx of collectors will augur a steep increase in the price of this material.

Another series is the so-called "broken bank bills." These are notes of banks that have failed which makes them, of course, not redeemable. There are quite a number of them and many may still be obtained in excellent condition. Their popularity will be increased and will probably follow the pattern of collecting U.S. broken bank notes which has been growing by leaps and bounds.

The last series I will mention are the Newfoundland notes. These are "Cash" notes issued from 1901 to 1914 in the following values: 25¢, 40¢, 50¢, 80¢, $1, $2, and $5.

It is said that these notes were used to provide funds for public works and road projects. All of them are scarce, especially in top condition.

In 1920, a $1 and $2 government issue was printed. These were the last of the notes issued by the colony.

Canadian Tokens

Along with the tokens of Australia, the United States, and other countries, there has been an increased interest and demand for the Tokens of Canada.

Back in the early days of Breton and Leroux, most collectors were assembling sets of the various tokens, including varieties, and this was the discussion at many of the club meetings and the subject of many articles.

I remember as a young man my correspondence with a number of famous Canadian collectors. A good deal of this was devoted to information on tokens. I corresponded with Mr. Reynaud, the famed curator of the Chateau de Ramezay collection. Varieties of tokens were discussed with regard to authenticity and whether they belonged in a Canadian collection, etc. Then, for many years the trend in numismatics was to the decimal series and speculative material, but more recently there has been a renewed interest in token collecting.

Rare Transportation Token of Canada
This piece was used as bridge fare for a horse drawn vehicle in Montreal.

When I first started collecting Canadian tokens, about forty years ago, the common material was available in coin shops in inexpensive foreign trays. Bidding in auctions in Great Britain, Belgium, the Netherlands, and France, I obtained many choice pieces seldom seen listed today. In all my years of collecting, I have found Canadian tokens to be one of the most challenging and fascinating fields.

It is not difficult to obtain the common pieces, so it is advisable for a novice in this field to try to acquire some of the semi-scarce or rare pieces if possible. Pieces that were rare forty years ago are very difficult to obtain today—pieces like the Sideview half-penny and penny, the Bridge or Bout de L'Isle tokens, the crude "Vexator Canadiensis," the Hunterstown, the Leslie &

Rare Canadian Token
Bank of Montreal, 1839 showing the famous side view

Sons 2 pence (which was called the "1799 large cent of Canada" because of its rarity and desirability).

Other pieces, such as the Northwest Company, are now also listed in the U.S. Catalog, since this company operated in what is now United States territory as well as in Canada. This token always comes holed and usually in rough condition. One piece in perfect condition is in the J. Douglas Ferguson collection.

Another rarity is the ship token dated 1858. A token on which the obverse has a Harp and the reverse "Ships Colonies & Commerce" is also listed among the blacksmith tokens. It is of special interest to collectors of this series.

The Lauzon Ferry, 1821, is a token sought after by both transportation collectors and regular collectors.

One unusual error in the Canadian token field is the token

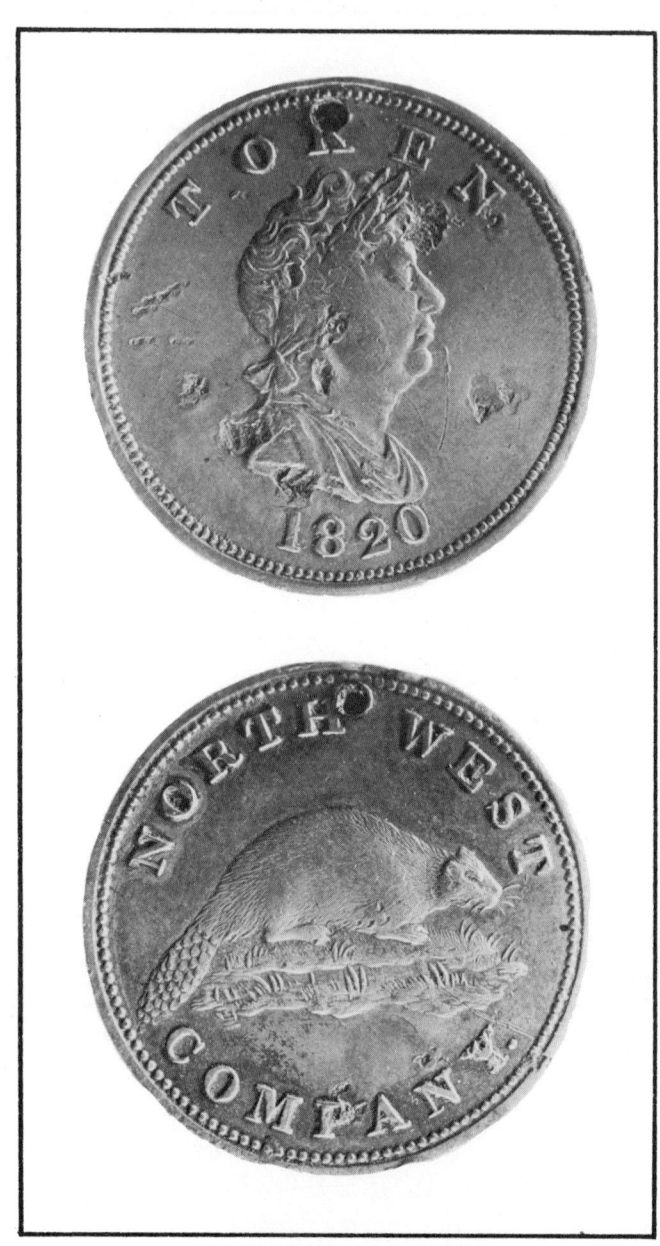

Northwest Company Token
Used in both Canada and the United States as an exchange to Indians and trappers for fur skins.

incorrectly dated *1382,* instead of *1832.* This piece always draws considerable comment and is much in demand.

Among the items which one should have no difficulty in obtaining are the Quebec Bank tokens. With few exceptions they are found in excellent condition.

Many of the Nova Scotia tokens are fairly common, as are some from Prince Edward Island and New Brunswick.

Newfoundland tokens are more difficult to obtain, except for the Rutherford pieces.

The Blacksmith Token of Canada

One of the ugliest and most badly struck of Canadian coins is the blacksmith token. The story of this piece is most unusual.

In the early 1830's, there was a shortage of hard money in Canada and to offset this, copper coins were accepted in bulk.

A Montreal blacksmith, who happened to be a heavy drinker, devised a method to pay for his dissipation. He prepared a die and struck coins that looked very crude—as though they had been in circulation.

Whenever he needed money and his thirst exceeded his finances, he struck two or three dollars worth of these coppers, and always had sufficient change for his needs. His method was crude, and his coins partially unreadable, but he achieved the results he wanted.

A number of varieties of these Canadian tokens are scarce and some of them are extremely rare.

The best known and most common variety—very crudely struck—shows a bust of George III on the face and on the reverse, Liberty seated.

* * *

The miscellaneous tokens present a challenge to the collector, since there are so many varieties, sizes, types, and along with the very common ones, those in the scarce or rare class.

Reprints of many of the out-of-print token publications are now available due to the newly awakened interest and demand.

X

The Royal Metal of Numismatics

Gold was one of the first metals known to man. For thousands of years, it has been one of the most important and highly prized of all substances. Universally recognized as a precious metal of high excellence, gold is unrivalled in color and lustre. Its fine qualities of preservation and ductility have enabled it to be fashioned into many objects of beauty and value—including money.

Seldom found in a completely pure state, gold usually contains other metals, especially silver. If the silver ratio is high, the alloy is known as electrum. This alloy is more suitable for minting coins than pure gold would be since it is more durable than gold itself.

The color variation in gold coins results from the different alloys used. Red gold consists of 75% gold and 25% copper. Green gold contains 25% silver. Blue gold has 25% iron.

In many countries—especially France and India—gold is hoarded. It is illegal to hoard gold in the United States, and there is no free domestic gold market. The coinage of virtually all gold coins was suspended in 1933.

The first regular United States gold issue was adopted in 1849, following the discovery of gold in California. The first $3 gold piece was struck in 1854, and despite the coin's lack of popularity—and the scant necessity for it—it was continued until 1889.

On March 6, 1933, President Franklin D. Roosevelt signed an executive order that stopped banks from paying out gold

United States $5 Gold Piece

and redeeming gold certificates without permission. Ever since, gold has been used exclusively in bullion form for reserve purposes. All imports, as well as newly-mined gold, must be sold to the Government.

Gold dollars were first struck in 1849, and were known as the Liberty head or small-sized type. The piece was soon made larger in diameter and thinner. Another design change was the

United States Gold Double Eagle

feather headdress, given to the Liberty Head which caused the piece to be known as the Indian Head or large-sized type. The design was changed again in 1856 by enlarging the head.

Other gold coins struck were double eagles ($20), eagles ($10), half eagles ($5), quarter eagles ($2.50), four dollars or "Stella," and three dollars.

The double eagle comes in two main varieties: Liberty with crown, and the Saint-Gaudens type with Liberty standing. A few experimental pieces of this type were struck with extra high relief, and 11,500 were later issued for general circulation.

One fine specimen of the extra-high relief variety brought over $18,000 at a sale in 1961. The regular high relief variety has thirteen rays extending from the sun, while the experimental variety has fourteen.

Because the Presidential order officially removed them from circulation, U.S. gold coins are scarce. The smallness of the remaining supply is reflected in the high premiums that most gold coins bring. That which is now left of a colorful segment of monetary history is being carefully and legally preserved.

Brasher Doubloon

One of the most sought-after and valuable of the world's coins is the Brasher doubloon.

Known even to the layman because it has been the subject of mystery novels, movies, and television presentations, and highly publicized for many years, even the mention of this gold piece is sure to generate interest and excitement.

Ephraim Brasher, a goldsmith and silversmith, struck these coins in 1787. When originally issued they were worth about $16. Today, only six specimens are known and four of them are owned by museums.

In the famed robbery of coin rarities from the Yale University numismatic collection, a Brasher piece was stolen. It was a pedigreed item that could not be sold to a collector or dealer and it was thought that someone might have melted it down for a few dollars worth of gold.

Fortunately, this piece was recovered and is now back in the Museum vaults, a rarity that escaped the melting pot.

Ephraim Brasher is also known for the finely wrought silver pieces he designed. His hallmark is prized by collectors.

* * *

Nowhere is the phrase "All is not gold that glitters" more applicable than in dealing with the small California gold pieces.

Brasher Doubloon

This piece is one of the world's most valuable coins.

Struck in denominations of one dollar, one-half dollar and one-quarter dollar, these coins were issued from 1852 until 1882, when the U.S. Government passed a law that forbade private coinage.

Issued in part because of a shortage of small change such as has happened several times in American history, these tiny coins come in both round and octagonal shapes and in hundreds of different varieties and types.

In recent years, many souvenir issues have appeared. Mostly put out by jewelers, these are usually only gold-plated without any real gold used in the piece at all. Many of these are copies of the genuine early California gold pieces and can be easily mistaken for the originals by a beginner.

One of the best methods of determining a genuine piece is by the words "Dol." or "Dollar" with the denomination on the reverse. These usually come with three different type heads: Liberty, Indian, and Washington head.

The Washington heads are quite rare and all of the $1 pieces are difficult to obtain, especially the round piece, the rarest item which sells for as much as $300 in Proof condition.

Being small and thin enough to be easily bent these pieces have, understandably, over the years disappeared or been mutilated—thousands were made into pieces of jewelry. Occasionally one can be seen even today in a bracelet or earring.

More recently, reproductions of these California items have been produced in fairly large quantities, for modern jewelry. Those in metals other than gold can be easily identified as not genuine.

Probably the most famous coin counterfeiter of all times was Josh Tatum, who, with the aid of a jeweler friend, gold-plated the 1883 Liberty Nickels and passed them off as five dollar gold pieces, which had the same size and appearance of the nickel.

Tatum's custom was to buy some five-cent item in a store,

hand the merchant a "gold piece" from which he would receive four dollars and ninety-five cents in change.

When Tatum was finally taken into court for fraud, the charges against him were dismissed because he had never asked for change. And it was because of his antics that the government changed the reverse of the nickel, replacing E PLURIBUS UNUM with the word CENTS.

At today's prices, Tatum might have been hard-pressed to find anything to buy for the proverbial nickel, but as it was, he managed to make approximately $15,000 with his "gold piece" scheme and that was quite a fortune for the period.

Gold Pieces of the Old West

Among the scarcest and most unusual series in numismatics are the private or territorial gold pieces.

Most of these were issued from the 1830's to the 1860's, by private bankers, assayers, and mining companies. They are all scarce and some—which are among the rarest items of numismatic Americana—bring prices well into five figures when offered for sale or at auction.

A great deal of the private gold pieces were issued because of the shortage of money in the various mining camps where pokes of gold dust were most commonly used and every saloon or general store had a scale for weighing out the amounts of gold needed for a purchase.

During the 1830's and 1840's, quite a bit of gold was mined in Georgia and North Carolina. The firms of Templeton Reid and the Bechtlers struck a number of gold coin pieces.

The Templeton Reid pieces are extremely rare. The 1849 $10 gold piece, a unique piece that was in the U.S. Mint collection, was stolen from a cabinet at the Philadelphia mint on August 16, 1858. To this day, mystery still surrounds this piece. Not only has it never been recovered, but nothing has been heard of it to the present time. There is some speculation that the thief perhaps melted the coin down for its bullion value.

A few of the Bechtler pieces are still obtainable, but some which are of extreme rarity are listed at from $3,000 to $5,000 each.

The greatest number of the gold pieces struck were from 1849 to 1860, after the discovery of gold in California. It was during the Gold Rush that this coinage began, and it then continued for a number of years.

Some of these pieces were struck into ingots. A Unique piece, probably the first struck in California, has the legend, CAL GOLD on the obverse and TEN DOLLARS on the reverse. This piece is thought to have been struck in San Francisco in 1849.

The ingots came in various shapes and sizes, some almost square, some oblong. Denominations vary depending on the weight of the gold. One struck by Meyers & Co. is an $18 ingot. Moffat Co. struck ingots with denominations of $9.43, $14.25, and $16. It is estimated that the $14.25 ingot is worth more than $10,000.

Many of the $50 "slugs" as they sometimes are called, are of the highest interest to gold collectors and eagerly sought. They break auction records each time they are featured in a sale.

Another well-known and extremely rare gold piece is the $10 Massachusetts and California Company item of 1849. It is thought that someone from Massachusetts went to San Francisco with the equipment necessary for coining gold but there is a good possibility that all of these pieces were struck in the east as patterns in preparation for a larger venture in California, for which the master plans were never completed and of which only the few patterns remain.

During the 1860's, Clark Gruber and Company, which originally started in Leavenworh, Kansas, in 1858, and operated a bank and mint, issued $10 and $20 gold pieces, as well as pieces in other denominations. One $20 piece has the legend, "Pikes Peak Gold Denver 20 D." and the reverse, "Clark Gruber & Company, 1860," with eagle in center. Dies and presses for this company's coins were hauled overland from Boston to Leavenworth by ox and mule teams—a hazardous journey in those days.

Clark Gruber & Co. Territorial $20 Gold Piece
These coins were privately minted during the boom gold period

Gold Certificates

Many collectors enjoy owning gold certificates. These were notes issued by the U.S. Government which stated they were redeemable in gold.

After December 28, 1933, collectors could not hold such currency legally, until the U.S. Treasury Department removed all restrictions on the holding of gold certificates, and while they may not now be redeemed for gold, they may be used for paper money collecting and display purposes.

The amazing total of $19,500,000 in gold certificates is outstanding. Thousands of these notes were hoarded over the years and there are even eight $10,000 gold certificates that have never been redeemed. There are only ten of the $5,000 denomination and 865 of the $1,000. Of the lower denominations, a great many still are held by the public or in collectors' hands.

The $100,000 bills were never released in circulation, but were used as a medium of exchange within the Federal Reserve Banks. This denomination is the highest ever used by the U.S. Government.

Treasury officials still hear from individuals who want to turn their gold certificates into gold pieces or gold bullion. Some seem amazed when they are notified that the statement on the notes cannot be honored. Notes sent in for redemption often come from foreign countries.

XI

Some Questions and Answers From the Coin Collector's Mail Bag

Over the years I have received thousands of letters from coin collectors, and the public, for information regarding their numismatic problems. The questions and answers which follow are those which have been most frequently asked and are usually the most troublesome to the novice.

Question: Someone showed me an old note and referred to it as a "Jackass note." Was the collector spoofing me?

Answer: No, the note which is commonly known as the "Jackass note" is the legal tender note issued in 1869, and in 1875, 1878 and 1880. This note has an eagle on the obverse and when turned upside town the eagle takes on the appearance of the head of a jackass. This is a desirable note and one sought by collectors.

Question: I recently saw a coin advertisement which listed an 1821 Spanish dollar and called it a "Pillar Dollar." I thought the Pillar Dollars were issued at an earlier period. Can you tell me about this?

Answer: You are correct. The real Spanish Pillar Dollars or 8 reales were issued from 1732 to 1772. These are the pieces of eight mentioned in the stories of pirates and the Spanish Main. The subsequent 8 reale pieces starting with 1774 had the portrait of the Spanish king on the obverse.

Question: Is there a United States $50 gold piece? A friend of mine told me he has seen one.

Answer: The only $50 gold piece issued is the commemorative coin called "The Panama Pacific" which was minted in 1915 at San Francisco. There were 483 pieces struck in a round shape and 645 were struck octagonal. They are usually found in special, deluxe cases. These coins are in demand by collectors of gold, commemoratives, and types. The catalog value of the round piece is $6250. The octagonal piece is listed at $4900.

Question: What are the terms "Pillars and Codfish" and "Sword in Hand" which I have heard applied to Colonial coins?

Answer: These terms do not apply to Colonial coins, but to the early Colonial notes issued before 1800. The Pillars and Codfish appear on some issues of 1776, 1778, and 1779 and are quite rare. The Sword in Hand reverse applies to some issues of 1775 and 1776, engraved by Paul Revere. The reverse show a military figure with Sword in Hand. Both of these notes are Massachusetts Colonial notes and are quite rare.

Question: Have you heard about varieties of the 1965 Canadian dollar?

Answer: There are five distinct varieties of the 1965 Canadian dollar that have become exceedingly popular. Only time will tell which of these varieties is the rarest.

Question: What is a three-legged Buffalo Nickel?
Answer: These Buffalo nickels were originally released and discovered in the Montana area. The nickname came about because a die became plugged, obliterating the midsection of the right foreleg, making it appear that the Buffalo is standing on three legs. These 5 cent pieces are extremely difficult to obtain in uncirculated condition and altered three-legged nickels exist—so beware. The fabrications usually leave a straight line where the lower leg has been removed from the upper. There are also minor varieties, including a so-called 2-1/2 legged Buffalo nickel.

Question: Was there a 20¢ denomination U.S. coin ever issued?
Answer: Yes. This is one of the most unusual of the U.S. obsolete coins. It was issued for only four years, in two of which these pieces were especially struck for the coin collector. The two rare dates are 1877 and 1878, with approximately 600 issued of each date.

The 1876 issue of the Carson City mint, which mint records show a coinage of 10,000, was never put into circulation and the pieces were melted down. However, fourteen of these pieces escaped the melting pot. These are extremely rare and found in museums and top collections only. Seldom offered for sale, they have a catalog value of $9000.

The 1875 date is the one usually found in collections. Coins were issued by the Philadelphia, Carson City, and the San Francisco mints. The San Francisco mintmark is the most common, with over a million pieces issued. The Philadelphia Mint piece is the scarcest, and the Carson City Mint, not quite as scarce.

United States 3¢ Silver Piece

Question: Is it true that the 1927 Commemorative Australian florin has a hand-made date?
Answer: Yes. This unusual coin has been individually engraved with the date and done by hand. The hand-engraving makes the coin very appealing to the collector.

Question: What are the smallest United States coins?
Answer: The U.S. silver 3¢ pieces which were issued from 1851 to 1873. These small silver coins were not too successful as they could be lost very easily and did not stack too well. There are three distinct types: Type 1 (issued from 1851 through 1853) has no lines bordering the six pointed star; Type 2 (issued from 1854 to 1859) has three lines; Type 3 (issued from 1860 to 1873) has only two lines. Except the 1851, of which 720,000 were made at the New Orleans Mint, all were minted at the

Philadelphia Mint. The New Orleans pieces are fairly scarce.

The greatest number were issued in 1852 and 1853 when 30,000,000 were made, but because the public did not like these coins, fewer and fewer were issued, until from 1864 to 1873, only token amounts were issued and those mostly for collectors.

The 1864 date is the rarest, with only 470 issued in Proof condition, and in 1873, only 600 were issued and these coins catalog at $275 and $200 each.

These should not be confused with the U.S. 3¢ nickel pieces issued from 1865 to 1889, which are the size of a dime.

Question: What is gun-money?
Answer: These were pieces issued in the 1680's which were made from captured cannon in Ireland. The coins are most unusual as they have as part of the date the month as well as the year.

Question: What are U.S. trade dollars and are they legal tender?
Answer: U.S. trade dollars were issued from 1873 to 1885, for circulation in the Orient to compete with Mexican and Spanish dollars circulating there. Originally, these coins were legal tender, but in 1876, after the decline in the price of silver bullion, they were no longer legal tender and were minted only in accordance with export demand.

Trade dollars of the U.S. never could seem to compete with the others and eventually—if not mutilated—were redeemed.

In 1877, some 13,000,000 were issued at the Philadelphia, Carson City, and San Francisco Mints. From 1879 to 1885, fewer than 2,000 were issued each year for collectors. In 1884, only 10 pieces were minted, while in 1885, the ridiculous number of 5 pieces were struck. When offered for sale in auctions, these two dates bring close to $10,000. The trade dollar is one of the most unusual and interesting of U.S. type coins.

Question: What was the first country to use copper in its coinage?
Answer: Rome was the first country to use copper. The Romans struck large quantities of coins in gold, silver, and copper. Hoards have been found in Italy, France, Africa, and other regions once part of the Roman Empire.

Question: Was tobacco ever a legal currency?
Answer: In 1618, the General Assembly of the Colony of Virginia passed an Act declaring tobacco a currency and the treasurer of the Colony was ordered to accept it at a fixed valuation.

Young girls imported into Virginia in 1620 and 1621 as wives for the colonists were valued at 100 pounds of tobacco each.

In 1642, a law was passed making tobacco the sole currency and forbidding contracts payable in money.

Question: I have heard of commemorative half-dollars. Were any U.S. commemorative dollars issued?
Answer: Yes. The so-called Lafayette dollar of 1900 which shows the heads of both Washington and Lafayette on the obverse is a commemorative piece. The equestrienne on the reverse is similar to the statue of General Lafayette that was erected in Paris as a gift of the American people. These coins originally sold for $2.00 but have increased in value a great deal.

Question: What is a "love token"?

Answer: This is a term used in numismatics in connection with U.S. and foreign silver coins that have been beautifully engraved by skilled craftsmen and jewelers with initials, names, etc. These coins were extremely popular in the 1880's and were used as bracelets, earrings, and pendants. Many of these coins are found with engravings, "Mother," "Father," "Sister," "Brother," and various names and initials, which when added to a bracelet, would give the wearer a coin for each member of the family. Usually coins with the names of sweethearts and friends were added. Many of the beautiful engravings depict animals, street scenes, and insignias of organizations.

The popularity of this kind of jewelry can be compared to that of the charm bracelet of today.

Question: What is the highest value note ever issued?

Answer: During the inflation in Hungary, 1945 to 1946, the 1,000,000,000,000,000,000 Szazmillio B. Pengo was issued. This is the highest denomination note known. The note reveals the inflated economy of the country following World War II.

Question: What was the first U.S. coin to carry the national motto, "In God We Trust"?

Answer: The U.S. two-cent piece, which was issued from 1864 to 1873, was the first to carry the motto. This coin was devised by Congress to remedy the severe shortage of small change resulting from the hoarding of coins during the Civil War. Approximately 20,000,000 pieces were minted in 1864 and 13,000,000 in 1865.

During 1866, '67 and '68, about 3,000,000 per year were coined and then they were issued in smaller numbers

1864 Two Cent Piece

until 1873, when only proofs were struck especially for collectors.

These coins were well received and were in constant use for many years.

Question: What determines the value of a coin?
Answer: It is a matter of supply and demand. A coin may be rare, beautiful, of original color, and have an interesting story, and yet it might bring a nominal price. There are not many U.S. coins struck with under 1,000 minted and yet some of these coins do not bring great prices, while certain Lincoln cents—because of the demand for them—are always being sold at unusually high prices.

An example is the 1914-d Lincoln cent in Uncirculated condition. This will bring a much higher price than an 1879-1883 trade dollar, of which fewer than 1300 were issued. Actually the question is how many pieces are available for sale, in relation to the number of people who want to buy them. Many times at auctions, coins will bring far more than they can be purchased for at a regular retail store, perhaps because some bidders get carried away in the excitement of bidding and offer more than the market value.

Question: What is a Feuchtwanger cent?
Answer: This is a coin minted in 1837 by Dr. Lewis Feuchtwanger, who produced a metal consisting of nickel, copper and some zinc. He suggested to Congress that his metal be substituted for copper and he produced some 1¢ and 3¢ pieces for distribution to congressmen and other notables to demonstrate the fine qualities of his coins. These well-struck coins are the size of our small cent. There is an eagle on the obverse and the date 1837. The reverse has the legend, "Feuchtwanger's composition," with the words "one cent" in a wreath.

In spite of Dr. Feuchtwanger's efforts, Congress never approved the use of these pieces for coinage.

Question: What is "coin glass"?
Answer: "Coin glass" was manufactured during the 1800's. The various pieces show impressions of several U.S. coins, particularly the liberty-seated types. Some pieces were, also issued at the time of the Chicago Columbian Exposition, held in 1892-'93, although these pieces are not as desirable as the earlier ones.

Coin glass is eagerly sought by collectors and, since pieces get broken and chipped, it is getting more difficult to obtain. Today, many gift and specialty shops carry modern copies of the glass, on trays, etc., with the various coins pictured as decoration.

Question: Is it possible to invest in any of the larger coin companies?

Answer: Several companies have received clearance from the Securities and Exchange Commission in Washington to offer their stock to the public, so that anyone who feels this might be a good investment can easily buy shares in these companies.

Question: Is it necessary to obtain a license to search for buried treasure?

Answer: Not unless the search is to be conducted on public lands, in which case, permission of the Department of the Interior may be required. If you should be fortunate enough to locate gold, the acquisition and possession is governed by the gold regulation which allows the collector to acquire and possess gold coins of recognized and special value to the numismatist, including all gold coins made prior to April 5, 1933.

A treasure license is not required to hold or sell silver bullion or coins, whether from buried treasure or other sources.

Question: Did Benjamin Franklin ever print paper money?
Answer: Benjamin Franklin printed paper money for the Province of Pennsylvania.

Franklin mentions in his writings that a controversy arose about paper money in the Province. The common people felt there was not enough money in circulation, while the wealthier citizens opposed any increase in the paper currency.

Franklin, remembering that when the first paper money had been issued, it had stimulated trade and employment, favored an increase. He became enthusiastic in his support and wrote and printed an anonymous pamphlet, "The Nature and Necessity of a Paper Currency." Ben Franklin wrote, "It was well received by the common people in general, but the rich men disliked it for it increased and strengthened the clamor for money and they, happening to have no writers among them that were able to answer it, their opposition slackened, and the point was carried by a majority in the house. My friends, there, who conceived I had been of some service, thought it a fit reward to employ me in printing the money; a profitable job and a great help to me."

He printed some of this currency himself and with his partner, D. Hall. These are the notes in great demand today by paper money collectors.

On the reverse of the notes is the famous slogan, "To counterfeit is death" with the denomination and the legend, "Printed by B. Franklin."

Panama-Pacific International Exposition "so-called dollar" commemorating the opening of the Panama Canal.

Question: What are "so-called dollars?"

Answer: This term applies to dollar-size medals commemorative of expositions, celebrations, and the like. These medals depict many historical events and have been issued since the 1820's. Many of the pieces were issued for expositions, such as the Columbian, the Pan-American and various World's Fairs, for which beautiful pieces in various metals were struck. The silver pieces are usually scarce and much more difficult to obtain than the bronze or copper.

Question: Was stainless steel ever used in coinage?

Answer: Yes, at least six countries—France, Italy, Albania, Turkey, Vatican City, and Costa Rica—have used stainless steel for coins because it is a durable metal, has a nice lustre, and is in plentiful supply.

Question: What do you suggest in insurance coverage to protect a coin collection?

Answer: I suggest a fine arts floater policy, listing a record of the prices of the coins and numismatic items you have in your collection. This will be a big help if you should have a loss of any kind.

So-Called Dollar of 1907 Commemorating Jamestown, Virginia

United States Half Cent of 1828

Question: I have read in many publications about United States half-cents. I have never seen one. Did such a denomination exist? Where could one be obained?

Answer: The United States half-cent was minted from 1793 to 1857 and is a well-known U.S. obsolete coin.

Actually, there are no common half-cents because the total minted is approximately 8,000,000 pieces. The early dates from 1793 to 1797 are especially difficult to obtain and are becoming rare in collectable condition. Some collect these by dates and varieties and they make unusual study in themselves. Such terms as "spiked chin," "inner circle O," "small 6 (stems)," "small 6, no stems," "large 6, stems," etc. show the various types of interesting varieties that are available. Most coin dealers have some of these pieces in stock for sale to collectors.

Question: What is the "Orphan Annie" dime?
Answer: "Orphan Annie" is a term given to the 1844 dime—quite a scarce coin. There were 72,500 minted, but almost all seem to have disappeared. There are many stories about this coin, including one that highwaymen obtained a westbound shipment, and buried it, and that the coins were never recovered.

Because of its scarcity and the publicity, this coin is a well-known one and sought by collectors.

Question: Did the Mormons have their own money?
Answer: Yes. The Mormons had paper money issued over a number of years, but the most famous Mormon money is the gold pieces issued in Salt Lake City, Utah, from 1849 to 1860. Most of the coins have clasped hands on them, which shows Strength through Friendship. Brigham Young was the originator of the Mint and the coinage system.

The pieces come in four denominations: $2-1/2, $5, $10 and $20. While none of the pieces are common, the $10 and $20 are exceedingly rare.

Question: Why is it that so many of the Philippine silver coins come so badly beaten and have a corroded look about them?
Answer: A great many Philippine silver coins, along with others, were dumped into Manila Bay to keep them from the Japanese in 1942. Many have been recovered, but corrosion had set in and they are sold today at reasonable prices as curiosities, since the average collector does not want them in poor condition.

Question: Why is it that the U.S. Columbian half-dollar, which is the earliest one issued in 1892 and 1893, still is available at a reasonable price, while many more recent half-dollars brings a great deal of money?

Answer: The Columbian half-dollar was highly prized by the many visitors to the Columbian Exposition, where this piece was sold for $1 each. There were approximately 2,000,000 issued over the two years and the unsold remainder was released for circulation at face value. Many of them were kept by families as curiosities, so that a good number of coin lots offered to dealers today contain at least one of the Columbian half-dollar, that had been carefully put away as a souvenir of the World's Fair.

Quite a number of the modern commemorative half-dollars had small mintages which were gobbled up by collectors. Without many available, the prices have steadily increased.

Question: Does the United States strike coins for other nations?

Answer: From 1876 to 1963, an astonishing 782 different coins have been struck for 36 countries. One of the reasons that the United States stopped striking coins for foreign governments was the U.S. coin shortage of 1964. The United States has again struck coins for foreign countries. One hundred thirty four different coins were struck for the Philippines, while other countries, like the Belgian Congo, Greenland, and France had only one issue struck in the U.S.A.

Question: Why are coins of Edward VIII dated 1936 difficult to obtain?

Answer: Because of Edward VIII's abdication, these coins were issued for a very short period. Coins, however, had been prepared for New Guinea, Fiji, and other overseas possessions. Most of these come with holes to make it easier for the natives to string them for easier handling.

Question: I have seen the term "elongated" used in regard to tokens. Would you explain this to me?

Answer: An "elongated" piece is made by putting a coin or token between two steel rollers, on which a design has been engraved. When the piece goes through the rollers, the coin will come out elongated or thin, with the design stamped on it. These were first used at the Columbian Exposition and since then have been very popular at fairs, expositions, for use in political campaigns, and as souvenirs.

A book entirely devoted to this subject has recently been published.

Elongated Coins

Question: What is the so-called "Grizzly Bear Coin"?

Answer: One of the most unusual U.S. commemorative half-dollars was issued in 1936 to mark the opening of the Oakland Bay Bridge in California. These coins were struck at the San Francisco Mint, a total of 71,424 pieces being issued.

This fifty-cent piece was designed by Jacques Schnier, a San Francisco artist. The obverse shows a large grizzly bear which explains the coin's nickname. The California grizzly bear pictured is Monarch the Second. This coin is popular with collectors catalogs at $22 in uncirculated condition.

Question: Could you give me any information about the 1953 Canadian coins which are listed "with shoulder strap" and "without shoulder strap"?

Answer: All of the various denominations of the 1953 Canadian coins come with and without the shoulder strap. The "strapless" coins (on which the Queen is represented wearing a gown without straps over the shoulders) were first prepared and issued. After a great deal of discussion, it was decided to prepare new sets of dies and shoulder straps were placed on the Queen's gown.

Variety collectors have also discovered that the 1955 cent comes without shoulder straps. From the small number found it has been determined that this is quite scarce.

Question: I brought home some Japanese invasion money when I returned from World War II. Are these pieces of any value?

Answer: Most of these items are fairly common, as millions of pieces were printed. It was natural for the servicemen to keep some for souvenirs.

A booklet recently published on Japanese invasion money has brought a great deal of interest to this series. There are a few varieties which might be more difficult to obtain, such as the invasion notes which were overprinted in red, "The Co-Prosperity Sphere, What is it Worth."

This message was overprinted on the notes after they were captured by General MacArthur's troops and then they were dropped behind the Japanese lines for propaganda purposes.

The Japanese, who were optimistic and expected to conquer great areas, had notes printed in Dutch, English, Spanish. Many were inscribed with propaganda messages.

Question: Could you suggest some interesting pieces for a collection of odd and curious money? I have always been fascinated by the unusual in coin collecting.

Answer: This unusual field has many possibilities for collectors, among which are silk, linen, velvet and leather money of Germany; wooden money of Austria; encased postage stamps of several countries besides the United States (Austria, Italy, and France); bamboo talley sticks from China; bullet money of Siam; feather money of Brazil; bean money of Japan; beetle money of Ecuador; boat money of Annam. Other possibilities could be the key and knife money of China, the axe money of Mexico; and shell money of New Guinea.

These are just a few of the many kinds of pieces which could be combined into a fascinating collection and exhibit.

Question: Why is the 1918-D over 7 overdate variety of the U.S. 5¢ piece so valuable?

Answer: Most of these coins went out into circulation, and in the worn or low grades, it is quite difficult to distinguish the overdate. This coin catalogs $215 in Very Good condition and $5200 if brand new.

Question: Is a Confederate bill rare?

Answer: All Confederate notes have a premium, though it may range from small to substantial. Their value depends on the date, denomination, and condition. Some of the early 1861 issues in the high values are quite rare. On the other hand, the $5 and $10 notes of 1864 are very common and can be purchased for approximately $1 in ordinary condition. Large hoards of these notes come to light from time to time.

Question: Is the so-called "date restorer" of benefit in the cleaning of various coins, especially Buffalo Nickels?
Answer: All that happens when the restorer is used is that the application of an acid brings out the date—temporarily. The real collector considers this a poor method of cleaning coins, and pieces in this condition, unless of a very rare date, are only worth about face value.

Question: Wouldn't it be easy to counterfeit the new "sandwich" U.S. coins?
Answer: The U.S. Government states that it should be extremely difficult to counterfeit the new coins, and has done much study and research to make them foolproof in this respect.

Question: What is Chinese cash?
Answer: The term, "Chinese cash," applies to the Chinese coins with square holes. These were issued during the Manchu Dynasty, 1644-1912. Many sewing baskets, pieces of furniture, clothing, and accessories had originals or copies of these coins sewn on as ornaments.

    The Chinese were quite advanced in coin production and from 1662 to 1722 had twenty-two mints in operation.

    The circular outline of the Chinese Cash is said by tradition to symbolize Heaven, while the square center represents the Earth. The center hole was put to good use, as the coins would be strung to facilitate handling and making change.

Question: I have heard that there are two varieties of the Peace dollar, but I cannot find them. Could you help me?

Answer: There are two major varieties of the Peace dollar which was issued from 1921 to 1935. The 1921 dollar was struck with a much higher relief than the other dates, and one way to distinguish the two varieties is by counting the number of rays between the tail of the eagle and the mountain top. The 1921 items have eight rays, while the balance of the dates have six, although there have been unverified reports of a few cases where some later dates did have seven rays.

Question: As a Canadian collector, I noted for many years the Northwest Company token of 1820 was always listed in the Canadian series. Why is this now listed in the U.S. catalogs?

Answer: Both the Canadian and U.S. collectors can be happy about this item as it belongs in both catalogs. This company operated in an area covered by the Northwest States of the United States and the Southwest area of Canada. The tokens were used by the company for the Indians who brought their furs into the trading posts.

These tokens usually come holed, as the Indians would carry them on a string or leather thong. Only one specimen in perfect condition is known. All of these pieces are quite rare.

Question: What is a Micro-S 1945-S dime and how can it be recognized?

Answer: The term "Micro" is obtained from the word "microscopic," and in this variety, the mintmark is much smaller and more minute than the normal S mintmark. This dime is a recognized variety and is listed in the Guide Book. It is very difficult to obtain in nice, uncirculated condition.

Question: As a stamp collector, I know a number of countries such as Israel and Switzerland have featured coins or numismatics on their stamps. Would any of the United States numismatic items fall into this category?

Answer: Yes, and this fact gives numismatics a very interesting and close relationship to philately. The broken bank bill of the Piscataque Exchange Bank of New Hampshire on the $10 note, pictures both Franklin and Washington in the same designs as those used on the 1¢ and 3 ¢ stamp issues of 1851. The $50 bill issued by the Fairhaven Bank had the 1851 Washington head which was also used on the $2 bill of the Mt. Vernon Bank.

The Franklin vignette also appears on the $5 Canal and Banking Company bill, as well as the $3 Bank of Manchester bill.

The Washington vignette appears on quite a number of different denominations of the Exchange Bank of Virginia, as well as the $50 Mississippi Union Bank Bill, the $20 Bank of Camden and others.

The Union Bank of Tennessee had a $1 bill which shows the eagle of the carrier stamps, with engraved date, January 2, 1843.

Both Franklin and Washington appear on the $10 Canal Bank Bill and are the same vignettes used in the 1¢ and 3¢ of 1851-57.

This type of collection is very unusual and has won many prizes when displayed at coin conventions.

Question: Were coins issued to honor General Douglas MacArthur?

Answer: The Philippine Government issued two coins in 1947 to mark their National Indpendence. A peso or silver dollar was struck and 1/2 peso or fifty-cent piece. Both of these coins have a large, shoulder-length profile of the

General. His name appears on both sides of the bust, and beneath is the date, October 20, 1944, the day that he waded ashore at Leyte to keep his famous promise, "I Shall Return."

Question: Where did the term "Canadian Whiskey tokens" originate?

Answer: The term refers to the importance of the Whiskey Trade in the early days of Canada, as emphasized on one of the scarcer Canadian tokens. This is the piece with a ship and Upper Canada on the face of the coin. The reverse has the legend, "Commercial Change 1821" and the words "Upper Canada" on a cask. A slightly different variety of the same token has the words "Jamaica Rum" on the cask.

Question: Are the $1 bills without the words "In God We Trust" scarce?

Answer: These bills are common and have little or no premium value, if any at all. Some incorrect information published in the newspapers led to rumors that had many people putting these bills away. Since most dealers have them in stock, they can be purchased for a nominal amount in crisp, uncirculated condition.

Question: Why is there such a shortage of U.S. silver dollars? I have been able to go to the bank and get them in the past, but now find I cannot obtain them unless I pay a premium.

Answer: An officer of the Federal Reserve Bank stated that during the past several years the demand for silver has consistently exceeded the supply and as the market price of silver rose rapidly, silver dollars were drained—chiefly for speculative purposes—from the Treasury stock, until

1880 Cartwheel or Silver Dollar

now there are less than 3,000,000 silver dollars on hand.
It is estimated there are 485,000,000 silver dollars outstanding so even if a great many have been melted, there remain many unaccounted for.

Question: What is a "Moon token"?
Answer: This is a private token issued by an enterprising coin dealer, which states, "Good for $1 (1 astron). Redeemable

for $1 (1 astron). At any store or bank on the moon until 12-31-69."

The dealer is optimistic as he expects us to be on the moon before 1970 and in business, but is to be commended because he does not want the coin collectors to be caught napping when we achieve our goal.

What seems like a fantasy today becomes the reality of tomorrow and with Moon tokens now being available, possibly we will have some issued for Mars, Venus, and other planets.

XII

■

Coin Values For the Collector and Investor

Coin Values

Almost every coin dealer or collector has heard someone say, "This coin is a hundred years old and has been in my family for many years. It is very rare." It is typical of the novice collector to believe that age is the dominant factor in determining the value of a coin. Actually, age has little to do with this. There are some 2,000 year old coins that can be purchased for as little as fifty cents because hoards of ancient coins continually come to light as digging continues in Italy, Greece, Syria, Israel, and many other countries.

Naturally pieces are found that are rare or even unknown in numismatic cabinets, but the great majority are common and there are more available pieces than there are purchasers for them. The law of supply and demand again creates a seemingly contradictory situation.

Several factors are taken into consideration in setting a value on numismatic material. The number of pieces minted is important, of course, although there are cases—as in some less popular series—in which low mintage coins can be purchased quite reasonably.

One of the most important considerations is the condition of the coin. Collectors want coins in the best possible condition. A knowledge of grading is of first importance, whether one is buying or selling. A U.S. coin of a certain date, for example, might be worth ten cents in Poor condition, fifty cents in Fair condition, fifty dollars in Extremely Fine condition, one hundred and fifty dollars in Uncirculated condition. With this in mind it is easy to see how important proper grading is.

There are several books on the grading of U.S. coins and one of these is necessary, whether you wish to buy or sell. Some of the terms used for classification are as follows:

PROOF COINS (PRF)

These are especially struck from polished dies and finished by hand. These coins, produced for coin collectors, are the finest condition obtainable and are always in demand.

UNCIRCULATED COINS (UNC)

These coins are brand new, show no wear and, never having been placed in circulation, are just as they came from the coining press.

EXTREMELY FINE (XF)

Very faint evidence of having been in circulation. Sometimes show some of the original lustre.

VERY FINE (VF)

Show a little wear on the high spots, but the coin is still in very sharp and desirable condition.

FINE (F)

Coins which have been in circulation, but retain all features distinctly and show no heavy scratches or nicks. The word "Liberty" is legible on most series and the coin is presentable in appearance.

VERY GOOD (VG)

A little below "fine" grade, but all lettering clear and bold.

GOOD (G)

The design and legend are plain and the date clear. The coin shows considerable wear and possibly has a few minute nicks or light scratches.

FAIR (FR)

The coin is well worn. Some of the letters may not be legible. Even though the coin shows a great deal of wear, the date should be clear.

POOR (PR)

These coins are not suited for the collector except in the instance of a scarce date or rare item, used perhaps for fillers until better specimens can be obtained.

There are many conditions in between those mentioned and others that modify them which are used to describe coins as fairly as possible. Adjectives such as Plugged, Holed, Nicked, Scratched, Dented, are used to give the most accurate possible description to the buyer.

The major descriptions given here should give some idea of what to expect when ordering or purchasing coins, or when offering them for sale.

The date of the coin is very important. For example, the U.S. 1856 Flying Eagle cent is very rare, while the 1857 Flying Eagle cent is fairly common. The 1856 U.S. large cent is common while the 1857 U.S. large cent is scarce. The 1799 large cent is the rarest date, while the 1793—the first year of issue—is not as difficult to obtain. This standard applies to the whole field of coin collecting, and it has taken one hundred years to establish the correct levels of scarcity and rarity of the material.

The following listing is made in two conditions: GOOD condition in which the coin may be worn but all lettering is readable; and UNCIRCULATED condition, in which the coin looks brand new, never having been placed in circulation.

Please remember that these prices are average, taken from the trends of the leading coin newspapers and quotations and prices from the leading catalogs. Prices fluctuate according to the supply and demand and what may be a badly wanted coin one year could be a piece which would not be of much interest the following year. In selling coins, it is important to remember that the dealer purchasing them has to allow for a reasonable margin of profit and there are times when he is overstocked on some material and cannot use it all.

American Coins

FLYING EAGLE CENT

	Good	Unc.
1856	$ 650.00	$2,250.00
1857	4.50	110.00
1858	4.75	135.00

COPPER NICKEL CENT

1859	3.00	80.00
1861	6.00	85.00
1862	1.75	25.00
1864	4.00	50.00

INDIAN HEAD CENT

1864 (*without* L on ribbon)	1.50	50.00
1864 (*with* L on ribbon)	13.00	225.00
1869 (over 8 [overdate])	40.00	675.00
1869	12.50	300.00
1870	12.50	150.00
1871	16.00	185.00
1872	18.00	250.00

		Good	Unc.
1875		$ 4.00	$ 75.00
1877		90.00	750.00
1880		1.00	22.50
1885		3.50	45.00
1890		.40	17.50
1904		.25	8.00
1908	(S)	15.00	100.00
1909	(S)	65.00	300.00

LINCOLN CENT

		Good	Unc.
1909	(vdb on rev.)	.75	5.00
1909	(S vdb)	100.00	225.00
1909	(S)	17.50	70.00
1910	(S)	2.50	40.00
1911	(S)	7.00	55.00
1911	(D)	1.00	30.00
1912	(D)	1.25	45.00
1912	(S)	3.50	45.00
1913	(D)	.75	40.00
1913	(S)	2.50	45.00
1914	(D)	35.00	550.00
1914	(S)	4.00	75.00
1915		.40	65.00
1915	(S)	3.00	40.00
1921	(S)	.50	160.00
1922	(D)	2.50	45.00
1923	(S)	1.00	225.00
1924	(D)	8.50	175.00
1924	(S)	.50	85.00
1926	(S)	3.00	100.00
1931	(D)	3.00	55.00
1931	(S)	20.00	60.00
1933	(D)	1.50	20.00

	Good	Unc.
1955 Double Die	$ 110.00	$ 375.00
1960 Small date	3.50	6.00

All common Lincoln cents are available in Uncirculated or brand new condition at reasonable prices.

TWO CENT PIECES

	Good	Unc.
1864	2.00	25.00
1872	35.00	125.00
1873 comes in Proof condition only		675.00

THREE CENT NICKEL

	Good	Unc.
1865	1.75	17.50
1875	5.00	40.00
1877 Rare, comes in Proof condition only		750.00
1878 Rare, comes in Proof condition only		250.00
1885	8.00	65.00
1887	15.00	100.00
1889	7.50	35.00

SHIELD 5¢ PIECE

	Good	Unc.
1866	5.50	125.00
1867 with rays on reverse	7.50	160.00
1867 without rays	2.50	30.00
1870	3.50	40.00
1871	30.00	200.00
1875	11.00	100.00
1877 only 500 issued, only issued in Proof condition		1,100.00
1878 only 2,350 issued only issued in Proof condition		275.00
1879	15.00	65.00
1880	18.00	75.00
1881	12.50	60.00
1883	3.00	30.00

		Good	Unc.
LIBERTY HEAD 5¢ PIECE			
1883	(without cents on reverse)	$ 1.00	$ 7.50
1883	(with cents)	4.50	40.00
1884		5.00	40.00
1885		55.00	275.00
1886		27.50	115.00
1887		2.50	30.00
1888		5.00	32.50
1892		3.00	32.50
1894		4.50	45.00
1900		.65	25.00
1909		.75	22.50
1912		.50	20.00
1912	(Denver Mint)	1.50	200.00
1912	(San Francisco Mint) 238,000 Minted	25.00	400.00

1913, only five pieces of this date are known. One of the rarities of U.S. numismatics. When offered this piece brings more than $40,000.00 at private sale or auction.

		Good	Unc.
BUFFALO 5¢ PIECE			
1913		1.00	7.50
1913	(Denver Mint)	2.50	22.50
1913	(San Francisco Mint)	5.00	40.00
1914	(Denver Mint)	15.00	100.00
1915		1.00	17.50
1915	(San Francisco Mint)	7.50	125.00
1917	(Denver Mint)	3.00	75.00
1918	(Denver Mint, overdate variety)	200.00	5,000.00
1919	(San Francisco Mint)	3.00	175.00
1921	(San Francisco Mint)	8.50	275.00
1925	(Denver Mint)	4.00	200.00

	Good	Unc.
1927 (San Francisco Mint)	$ 1.25	$ 250.00
1931 (San Francisco Mint)	5.00	60.00
1937 (Denver Mint, 3 legged variety)	30.00	250.00

There are also sub-varieties of this coin, such as the 2-1/2 legged, etc.

| 1938 (D over S. This was discovered only a few years ago.) | | 30.00 |

JEFFERSON NICKEL

1938 (Denver Mint)	1.00	6.00
1938 (San Francisco Mint)	1.50	7.50
1939 (Denver Mint)	4.00	50.00
1939 (San Francisco Mint)	1.00	12.00

During the war years, 1942 through 1945, nickel was needed a great deal more than silver and the five cent pieces were struck with a 35% silver composition. With the increase in value of silver, the coins became worth more than the face value and tons of them have been melted for the bullion value.

1950 (Denver Mint)		17.50
1951 (San Francisco Mint)		6.00
1955		3.00

HALF DIME

1794	175.00	1,500.00
1795	125.00	700.00
1796	125.00	1,000.00
1797 (there are 3 varieties) (this date comes with 13/15/16 stars)	150.00	1,100.00
1802	1,000.00	8,500.00

(this date is the most sought after one in half-dime series collecting and is Rare in any condition)

		Good	*Unc.*
1829		$ 6.00	$ 70.00
1837	(Liberty cap)	4.00	65.00
1837	(Liberty seated)	50.00	250.00
1838	(New Orleans Mint)	50.00	450.00
1838		2.50	45.00
1839		2.50	40.00
1846	(27,000 minted)	45.00	250.00
1849		2.00	35.00
	The 1849 comes with 2 overdates		
1849	(O) New Orleans Mint	22.50	225.00
1853	(without arrows)	10.00	75.00
1853	(O) (without arrows)	55.00	375.00
1853	(with arrows)	2.50	45.00
1858		2.00	30.00
1863		12.50	85.00
1867	(low mintage, 8,625)	10.00	85.00
1868	(San Francisco Mint)	3.00	30.00
1872		1.75	30.00
1872	(San Francisco Mint)	2.00	30.00

U.S. DIME

		Good	*Unc.*
1796		300.00	2,050.00
1797		200.00	1,675.00
1800		100.00	700.00
1804	(comes 13 and 14 stars on reverse)	150.00	1,250.00
1805	(comes with 4 berries and 5 berries)	75.00	500.00
1808		45.00	375.00
1820		10.00	125.00
1823	(over 22—this year comes with small e's and large E's legend)	12.50	150.00
1829	(comes with small, medium and large 10¢ on reverse)	8.00	100.00

		Good	*Unc.*
1834		$ 5.00	$ 100.00
1837	(draped bust type)	3.50	100.00
1837	(Liberty seated)	45.00	350.00
1838	(comes with small stars, large stars, and partial drapery)	6.00	75.00
1841	(New Orleans Mint)	2.00	65.00
1844	(this scarce date has been nicknamed 'Orphan Annie' is difficult to obtain and sought by collectors)	25.00	300.00
1846		12.50	150.00
1853	(without arrows at date)	20.00	100.00
1853	(with arrows)	2.00	45.00
1856	(San Francisco Mint)	22.50	300.00
1860	(O, New Orleans Mint)	60.00	800.00
1871	(CC, Carson City Mint)	150.00	1,500.00
1872	(CC, Carson City Mint)	75.00	750.00
1873	(CC, Carson City Mint without arrows. Only one piece known)		
1873	(CC, Carson City Mint, with arrows)	350.00	1,500.00

The arrows indicate the change in weight of the coinage and were only used for 2 years, 1873 and 1874.

1874	(with arrows)	10.00	125.00
1874	(San Francisco Mint)	15.00	150.00
1875	(CC, this date comes with the mintmark under the wreath and in the wreath on the reverse of the coin)	3.00	40.00
1877		1.50	25.00
1880		10.00	55.00
1886		7.50	50.00

	Good	Unc.
1891	$ 1.50	$ 22.50
1891 (O) New Orleans Mint)	2.75	35.00
1891 (San Francisco Mint)	2.50	35.00

LIBERTY HEAD TYPE DIME

	Good	Unc.
1892	1.00	22.50
1892 (O, New Orleans Mint)	2.50	35.00
1892 (S, San Francisco Mint	16.00	100.00
1894 (O, New Orleans Mint)	22.50	275.00
1894 (S) mint records show that only 24 of these were coined. They are seldom offered, even at auction, and have brought as much as $13,000 and probably now have a value of $15,000.		
1895 (O)	40.00	600.00
1895 (S)	6.00	115.00
1896	2.50	25.00
1897	.75	22.50
1898 (S)	2.50	75.00
1901	.50	20.00
1901 (S)	15.00	400.00
1905 (O)	1.00	55.00
1911 (S)	.75	30.00
1916 (S)	.25	17.50

MERCURY TYPE DIME

	Good	Unc.
1916	.25	7.00
1916 (D, Denver, the key date of this series,	90.00	700.00
1916 (S, San Francisco)	.75	15.00
1921	10.00	300.00
1921 (D)	15.00	275.00
1926 (S)	4.50	300.00

	Good	Unc.
1931 (D)	$ 4.00	$ 60.00
1931 (S)	2.50	50.00
1931	1.00	27.50
1942 (over 41 overdate)	65.00	500.00

ROOSEVELT TYPE DIME

	Good	Unc.
1949		7.50
1949 (S)		10.00
1950 (S)		8.00
1951 (S)		7.50

TWENTY CENT PIECE

Twenty cent pieces were only minted for four years, 1875 through 1878. They were similar enough to the quarter dollar in appearance to cause many errors in making change.

	Good	Unc.
1875	22.50	150.00
1875 (CC, Carson City)	25.00	175.00
1875 (S)	20.00	140.00
1876	27.50	175.00

1876 (CC) Although the mint records show 10,000 minted, this is one of the scarcest U.S. coins. Occasionally offered at auction, this coin should be worth approximately $10,000.

The 1877 and 1878 come in Proof condition only and were especially made for the collector. Approximately 500 were made each year. The estimated value is $500. per coin.

QUARTER DOLLAR

	Good	Unc.
1796	700.00	5,500.00
1806 (over 5)	55.00	700.00

QUARTER DOLLAR CAPPED BUST TYPE

With bust facing left

	Good	Unc.
1815	20.00	500.00
1819 (lg. 9)	17.50	400.00

		Good	Unc.
1820	(sm.o)	$ 17.50	$ 350.00
1820	(lg.O)	17.50	350.00
1823	(over 22)	600.00	—
1827	(original, only 6 or 7 specimens are known		
1831	(sm. let.)	7.00	200.00
1831	(lg. let.)	7.00	200.00
1836		8.50	175.00
1838		8.50	175.00

LIBERTY SEATED QUARTER

		Good	Unc.
1838	(no drapery from elbow)	6.00	100.00
1839	(no drapery from elbow)	5.00	90.00
1840	(with drapery)	5.00	90.00
1841		12.50	110.00
1842	(O, New Orleans Mint) (Sm. Dt)	12.50	90.00
1842	(O, New Orleans Mint) (Lg. Dt)	5.00	60.00
1846		3.50	50.00
1849	(O)	60.00	500.00
1853	(O)	7.50	175.00
1853	(with arrows)	5.00	175.00
1855	(O, with arrows)	35.00	400.00
1859	(S)	22.50	200.00
1859	(O)	4.00	40.00
1859		3.00	35.00

1866 without motto above eagle. This unique piece brought $24,500 at a 1961 auction and would probably bring a great deal more if offered for sale again.

		Good	Unc.
1866	(with motto "In God We Trust" above eagle)	5.00	45.00
1870	(CC, Carson City)	115.00	800.00
1872		2.50	40.00

	Good	Unc.
1872 (CC)	$ 150.00	$ 1,000.00
1872 (S)	12.50	100.00
1873 (CC)	400.00	1,200.00
1873 (with arrows at date)	17.50	175.00
1873 (CC, with arrows)	300.00	1,800.00
1873 (S, with arrows)	22.50	150.00
1874 (with arrows)	20.00	175.00
1877	2.00	30.00
1877 (CC)	3.25	35.00
1878 (S)	135.00	850.00

The Quarter Dollars minted at the Philadelphia Mint from 1879 to 1889 are all low mintages, the highest mintage being 16,300 in 1822. All of these dates are scarce and desirable.

LIBERTY SEATED QUARTER

1879	17.50	70.00
1882	15.00	70.00
1885	16.00	67.50
1889	15.00	65.00

LIBERTY HEAD TYPE QUARTER DOLLAR

1892	.85	30.00
1892 (O)	2.50	40.00
1892 (S)	9.00	140.00
1896 (S)	90.00	1,250.00
1901 (S)	235.00	2,000.00
1909 (O)	10.00	300.00
1913 (S)	90.00	1,250.00
1916	.75	35.00
1916 (D)	.60	35.00

STANDING LIBERTY QUARTER DOLLAR

1916 52,000 minted	250.00	950.00
1919	4.00	50.00
1919 (D)	25.00	250.00
1919 (S)	28.50	325.00

	Good	Unc.
1921	$ 22.50	$ 250.00
1923 (S)	30.00	200.00
1927 (S)	5.00	650.00

WASHINGTON HEAD QUARTER DOLLAR

	Good	Unc.
1932	.50	12.50
1932 (D)	22.50	225.00
1932 (S)	22.50	100.00
1936 (D)	1.50	250.00

HALF-DOLLAR

	Good	Unc.
1794	250.00	10,000.00
1795	125.00	2,750.00
1796 (15 or 16 stars, both are approximately the same value)	1,500.00	7,500.00
1801	75.00	1,200.00

TURBAN HEAD HALF-DOLLAR

	Good	Unc.
1807 (small stars)	20.00	400.00
1807 (large stars)	17.50	325.00
1808	10.00	125.00
1814	10.00	125.00
1821	7.00	80.00
1831	6.00	55.00
1836 (lettered edge)	6.00	55.00
1836 (reeded edge)	45.00	325.00
1837 (reeded edge)	10.00	150.00

1838 (O. As far as has been ascertained only 20 of these were struck.) Brought $14,000 in 1967 auction sale.

	Good	Unc.
1839 (O)	50.00	300.00

LIBERTY SEATED HALF-DOLLAR

	Good	Unc.
1839 (no drapery from elbow)	25.00	350.00
1839	10.00	100.00
1844	4.50	65.00
1852	22.50	250.00
1853 (with arrows)	7.50	250.00

		Good	Unc.
1855	(S)	$ 32.50	$ 400.00
1858		3.50	50.00
1865		5.00	60.00
1870	(CC)	45.00	600.00
1874	(with arrows)	13.50	200.00
1874	(CC, with arrows)	30.00	500.00
1874	(S, with arrows)	22.50	250.00
1878	(S)	275.00	2,750.00

All of the half-dollars dated from 1879 to 1889 are extremely small mintages, the largest mintage being 12,833 in 1888.

		Good	Unc.
1879		40.00	85.00
1884		37.50	90.00
1886		62.50	125.00

LIBERTY HEAD HALF-DOLLAR

		Good	Unc.
1892		4.00	90.00
1892	(O)	22.50	100.00
1892	(S)	25.00	150.00
1896	(S)	20.00	300.00
1913		15.00	175.00
1914		20.00	250.00
1915		15.00	225.00
1915	(D)	1.50	90.00
1915	(S)	1.75	90.00

LIBERTY WALKING HALF-DOLLAR

		Good	Unc.
1916		6.00	90.00
1916	(D, mintmark on obverse)	5.00	70.00
1916	(S, mintmark on obverse)	17.50	175.00
1917		1.00	25.00
1917	(D, mintmark on obverse)	5.00	90.00
1917	(D, mintmark on reverse)	2.50	125.00
1917	(S, mintmark on obverse)	6.00	400,00
1917	(S, mintmark on reverse)	1.25	110.00
1921		25.00	600.00

	Good	Unc.
1921 (D)	$ 45.00	$ 800.00
1921 (S)	6.50	900.00
1938 (D)	20.00	175.00

FRANKLIN HALF-DOLLAR

	Good	Unc.
1948		10.00
1949		22.50
1953		12.50
1958		3.00

KENNEDY HALF-DOLLAR

	Unc.
1964	1.25
1964 (D)	1.25

SILVER DOLLAR

1794   1,200.00   12,000.00

1795 This coin comes with 2 leaves or 3 leaves beneath each wing of the eagle, both are of approx. the same value   175.00   1,200.00

1796   125.00   1,100.00

1797 comes with several varieties; 9 stars left and 7 right, with small letters; also, 9 stars left and 7 right with large letters; and 10 stars left and 6 on the right. All are of approximately equal value   150.00   1,250.00

1798, 1799 and 1800 come with many varieties, some scarcer than others.

1803   70.00   600.00

1804 This is one of the most valuable coins in the world, and is called the king of American coins.

GOBRECHT DOLLAR

The Gobrecht pieces were trial coins struck in very small quantities. It was decided not to strike them in large quantities for circulation. All of the pieces are rare and in demand. They come with the dates 1836, 1838, and 1839.

	Good	Unc.
1836 (plain edge, with C. Gobrecht on base)	$ 375.00	$1,200.00

LIBERTY SEATED SILVER DOLLARS

	Good	Unc.
1840	15.00	150.00
1846 (O)	15.00	150.00
1850	60.00	250.00
1853	40.00	250.00
1864	35.00	150.00
1871 (CC)	250.00	2,000.00
1872	15.00	75.00
1872 (CC)	140.00	1,100.00

LIBERTY HEAD SILVER DOLLAR

With all the interest in silver dollars during the last few years, many new varieties have come to light. Others will undoubtedly be discovered.

	Good	Unc.
1879		3.50
1885 (CC)		60.00
1886 (S)		35.00
1892 (CC)		45.00
1893 (S)	150.00	4,500.00
1921		3.00
1921 (D)		5.00
1921 (S)		5.00

PEACE DOLLAR

1921	30.00
1923 (D)	9.00
1924 (S)	40.00
1926 (S)	10.00
1928	90.00
1934 (S)	250.00

U.S. TRADE DOLLAR

	Good	Unc.
1873	$ 12.00	$ 125.00
1873 (CC)	17.50	225.00
1873 (S)	12.50	125.00
1877	12.50	75.00
1878 comes in Proof condition only. 900 minted.		400.00

All of the dates from 1879 to 1885 were issued in Proof condition only, the highest mintage being 1,987 in 1880. Only ten specimens were struck of the 1884, and only five pieces are known of the rarity, 1885. The dates from 1879 through 1883 have an estimated value of $350 each and the 1884 and 1885 are estimated at approximately $10,000 each.

Many of the trade dollars which circulated in the Orient, come with chopmarks, which Chinee merchants placed upon them after checking the coin for the genuineness of its silver content. The value of these chopmark coins depends on the number of chopmarks, and the condition of the coin. Under normal conditions they would be worth half of the regular prices.

U.S. COMMEMORATIVE GOLD

Coins in Very Fine condition should have the word LIBERTY completely legible and the knobs on coronet clear. The Uncirculated condition should be brand new with the original lustre.

$1

	Very Fine	Unc.
1922 Grant Memorial $1 with star	150.00	300.00
1922 Grant Memorial $1 without star	150.00	325.00
1904 Lewis & Clark $1	150.00	375.00
1903 Louisiana Purchase with Jefferson portrait	45.00	110.00

		Very Fine	Unc.
1903	Louisiana Purchase with McKinley portrait	$ 45.00	$ 110.00
1916	McKinley Memorial	35.00	80.00
1915	San Francisco Panama Pacific Exp.	35.00	75.00

$2.50

1915	San Francisco Panama Pacific Exp.	150.00	300.00
1926	Sesquicentennial	27.50	60.00

$50

1915	San Francisco Panama Pacific, round	3,000.00	5,500.00
1915	(S) San Francisco Panama Pacific, octagonal	2,750.00	4,500.00

These are the largest denomination U.S. coins issued.

U.S. GOLD

$1

1849	(Open wreath)	35.00	75.00
1849	(closed wreath)	35.00	72.50
1849	(C, Charlotte Mint, closed wreath)	150.00	500.00

1849 (C, open wreath) Only 2 specimens are known. They bring more than $5,000 when offered at auction.

1849	(D, Dahlonega Mint)	225.00	350.00
1849	(O, New Orleans Mint)	40.00	65.00
1853		40.00	55.00
1854	(D)	275.00	600.00
1855	(D)	1,250.00	2,500.00
1861	(D)	3,500.00	6,250.00
1880		150.00	275.00
1889		80.00	100.00

$2.50

1796	(without stars)	4,500.00	7,000.00
1796	(with stars)	5,000.00	8,000.00

	Very Fine	Unc.
1798	$ 2,000.00	$ 4,500.00
1804 (comes with 2 different reverses, one with 13 stars and one with 14 stars. Both have approximately the same value)	850.00	2,000.00
1808	4,000.00	6,000.00
1821	850.00	2,000.00
1831	500.00	900.00
1834 (without motto)	90.00	175.00
1839 (O, New Orleans Mint)	200.00	400.00
1843	60.00	90.00
1848	500.00	1,000.00

The 1848 Quarter Eagle is known with the counterstamp CAL. for California. These are very rare. Beware of counterfeits.

1848 CAL. counterstamp	3,000.00	5,500.00
1853	40.00	60.00
1854 (S, only 246 coined)	4,000.00	6,000.00
1864	300.00	450.00
1872	125.00	225.00
1880	150.00	250.00
1896	50.00	75.00
1907	45.00	65.00

INDIAN HEAD $2.50 U.S. GOLD

1908	30.00	40.00
1911 (D) the only scarce date of the Indian Head Type	300.00	400.00
1915	30.00	35.00
1929	27.50	35.00

Many of the $2.50 gold pieces were minted in very small quantities and because quite a few pieces were destroyed and used for jewelry, some dates are rarer than most collectors think.

U.S. $3 GOLD

1854	200.00	300.00

		Very Fine	*Unc.*
1854	(D, Dahlonega)	$ 1,500.00	$ 2,500.00
1854	(O, New Orleans)	225.00	350.00
1855	(S, San Francisco)	235.00	450.00
1862		225.00	325.00
1875	only 20 struck in Proof condition. Auction records of		20,000.00
1876	45 struck in Proof condition only. Worth close to		10,000.00
1882		275.00	475.00
1885		350.00	650.00
1889		300.00	450.00

U.S. $4 GOLD

These coins are called "Stellas" by collectors, and are Pattern coins—they were not issued for general circulation. They are known in several other metals besides the gold and all are very rare and desirable. They were only issued in 1879 and 1880.

U.S. $5 GOLD

1795	(small eagle on reverse)	$1,700.00	$2,250.00
1795	(large eagle on reverse)	2,250.00	5,000.00
1797	(15 stars or 16 stars, both with approx. the same value)	1,600.00	3,500.00
1799		500.00	900.00
1804	(comes with small 8 or large 8 in date)	500.00	700.00
1807		475.00	650.00
1812		400.00	600.00
1815	only 635 minted, estimated valuation of $6,000.		
1822	only 3 known-extremely rare		
1821		2,500.00	6,000.00
1829	(small date) This coin brought $21,500. at auction.		
1833		800.00	1,750.00
1834	(comes with a plain 4 and crosslet 4, both are very scarce		

		Very Fine	*Unc.*
	and have approx. the same value)	$ 900.00	$ 2,000.00
1837		80.00	175.00
1843		40.00	85.00
1849	(C, Charlotte Mint)	125.00	225.00
1849	(D, Dahlonega Mint)	125.00	225.00
1854	(S, San Francisco) has brought as much as $16,500 at auction.		
1866		300.00	425.00
1874	(CC, Carson City Mint)	200.00	375.00
1878		32.50	45.00
1878	(S)	32.50	45.00
1889		225.00	350.00
1898		27.50	35.00
1906	(D, Denver)	27.50	35.00
1908		25.00	35.00

U.S. INDIAN HEAD $5 GOLD

1908		30.00	40.00
1908	(D, Denver)	30.00	40.00
1908	(S, San Francisco)	160.00	350.00
1909	(O, New Orleans Mint) scarcest mintage of the Indian Head Type	300.00	450.00
1915		30.00	40.00
1929		1,200.00	1,500.00

U.S. $10 GOLD

1795		1,350.00	2,500.00
1796		1,150.00	2,500.00
1800		650.00	1,000.00
1804		850.00	1,500.00
1838		500.00	900.00
1840		85.00	175.00
1841	(O, New Orleans)	450.00	750.00

		Very Fine	*Unc.*
1845		$ 60.00	$ 165.00
1855		47.50	90.00
1858		3,500.00	5,500.00
1860	(S, San Francisco)	300.00	500.00
1870	(CC, Carson City)	275.00	450.00
1879		37.50	65.00
1881	(O, New Orleans)	85.00	145.00
1881	(CC, Carson City)	57.50	110.00
1881	(S, San Francisco)	37.50	47.50
1881		32.50	47.50
1900		32.50	75.00
1906	(D, Denver)	35.00	50.00

The 1907 Eagle is one of the most attractive of U.S. gold coins. This coin comes with a wire edge rim and periods before and after the legends. It is quite rare, since only 500 were minted. The same date with *no stars on the edge* is the rarest item as there is only one piece known.

Another rare piece is the 1907 *with the rolled edge and periods,* as only 42 pieces were minted.

1907	(without periods)	50.00	75.00
1909		55.00	70.00
1911	(S)	100.00	150.00
1915	(S)	160.00	250.00
1926		50.00	70.00
1930	(S)	2,250.00	4,250.00

U.S. $20 GOLD

This coin was first struck in 1849. There is only one specimen for that year which is in the Government collection at the Smithsonian Institute in Washington, D.C.

1850		135.00	400.00
1850	(O, New Orleans)	135.00	375.00
1854	(S, San Francisco)	135.00	285.00

	Very Fine	Unc.
1856 (O, New Orleans)	$ 3,250.00	$ 5,500.00
1866	87.50	150.00
1870 (CC, Carson City)	6,500.00	9,000.00
1875	75.00	135.00
1879 (O, New Orleans)	600.00	900.00

The dates 1883, 1884, and 1887 were issued in Proof only from the Philadelphia Mint. These are all very valuable numismatic items.

1903	75.00	135.00
1907	67.50	90.00
1907 (D, Denver)	67.50	92.50
1907 (S, San Francisco)	67.50	90.00

Many say the $20 gold piece of 1907 with the Flying Eagle is the most beautiful coin issued by the U.S. Mint. This famous gold piece was designed by the noted sculptor, Augustus St.-Gaudens. These coins would not stack properly and for that reason they were discontinued. Several of the varieties are all but impossible to obtain. The extra high relief pieces with lettered edge have auction records of over $18,000. The extra high relief with the plain edge is unique and not available.

The variety with the *large letters* on the edge comes in Proof only and is *unique*.

The two varieties which are obtainable are the *high relief roman numerals with the wire rim* and the *high relief with the flat rim*. These are both worth approximately the same amount.

1907 (Roman Numerals High Relief or Flat Rim Relief)	$ 500.00	$ 900.00
1909 (S, San Francisco)	65.00	87.50
1913	72.50	95.00
1913 (D, Denver)	70.00	95.00
1913 (S, San Francisco)	165.00	300.00
1927 (D, Denver)	2,250.00	4,750.00
1932	700.00	1,800.00

The last item in this listing of U.S. Coins is the commemorative type, first issued at the Columbian Exposition in 1892. Each piece is historical and is a kind of material which is collected by numismatists all over the world. There have been no commemorative half-dollars issued since 1954, but it is hoped that one day the Government will again strike these historical and unusual pieces. Most of these coins are collected in Uncirculated condition, although used coins may occasionally be found. The values listed will be for Uncirculated condition only.

COMMEMORATIVE HALF-DOLLARS

1892	Columbian	$ 7.00
1893	Columbian	4.00
1918	Illinois	20.00
1921	Pilgrim	19.00
1926	Sesqui-Centennial	13.00
1935	Spanish Trail	185.00
1936	Albany	45.00
1936	Elgin	40.00
1937	Roanoke	25.00
1938	New Rochelle	60.00
1946	Booker T. Washington—Set of 3 Mints, Philadelphia, San Francisco and Denver, the Set	9.00
1951	Washington Carver Set of 3 Mints, as above	15.00

The only Commemorative Quarter Dollar is the Isabella coin issued at the Columbian Exposition in 1893. This is the only U.S. coin with a portrait of a foreign monarch, Queen Isabella of Spain.

Commemorative Quarter, 1893, Isabella   85.00

The Lafayette Dollar was issued in 1900 and the heads of Washington and Lafayette appear on the obverse of this coin. On the reverse is a statue similar to a monument in Paris. This monument was presented to the French people for the great work and effort by the General in helping us to obtain our independence.

Lafayette Commemorative Dollar, 1900   150.00

CANADIAN COINS

Popularity polls prove that Canadian coins are near the top of the list and are much in demand throughout the world. Compared to the United States, Great Britain, Mexico and other countries, the coinage of Canada is comparatively recent as the first coins were struck in 1858, a little over a hundred years ago. Most Canadian catalogs and dealers start their grading with Very Good condition, but I personally feel they should use the Good grade, the same as we do here for the U.S. This is the condition where, although details may be worn, all the lettering is clear.

	Good	Unc.
CANADIAN LARGE CENT		
1858	$ 22.50	$ 85.00
1859	.85	17.50
1882 (Heaton Mint)	1.25	12.50
1892	2.50	20.00
1901	1.00	12.50
1907	1.25	12.50
1907 (Heaton Mint)	6.50	65.00
1919	.35	7.00
CANADIAN SMALL CENT		
1922	5.50	70.00
1923	12.00	175.00
1937	.05	2.50
CANADIAN 5¢ SILVER		
1858	6.00	65.00
1871	3.50	60.00
1875 (Heaton Mint)	20.00	400.00
1884	20.00	475.00
1892	1.50	40.00
1900 (oval O)	1.00	22.50
1900 (round O)	9.00	70.00
1911	1.50	35.00
1921 (the rarest 5¢ piece of Canada)	400.00	3,000.00

CANADIAN 5¢ NICKEL	Good	Unc.
1922	$ .15	$ 25.00
1925	20.00	375.00
1930	.15	35.00
1942	.10	25.00
1942 (Tombac)	.50	3.00
1944 (Steel)	.10	2.50
1947 (Dot) (Variety)	1.00	60.00

CANADIAN 10¢		
1858	4.00	115.00
1871	5.00	150.00
1875 (Heaton Mint)	40.00	1,000.00
1886 (comes with a small 6 and large 6 variety, both worth approximately the same	4.50	150.00
1913 (small leaves)	.75	45.00
1913 (broad leaves)	20.00	800.00
1932	.25	45.00
1948 (lowest mintage of the modern Canadian dimes	4.50	75.00

CANADIAN 20¢		
1858	30.00	350.00

Canadian twenty cent pieces were only issued in one year; 750,000 were minted, but the great majority were withdrawn from circulation and melted. This piece is needed in all type sets as well as date sets.

CANADIAN 25¢		
1870	4.50	125.00
1872 (Heaton Mint)	1.50	125.00
1885	15.00	450.00
1891	9.00	325.00
1904	3.50	300.00
1915	4.50	450.00
1927	6.00	400.00

	Good	Unc.
1937	$ .50	$ 20.00
CANADIAN HALF-DOLLAR		
1870	8.00	375.00
1871 (Heaton Mint)	22.50	650.00
1890 (Heaton Mint)	125.00	4,750.00
1900	7.00	350.00
1911	8.00	800.00
1917	1.50	225.00
1921 (one of Canada's rarest items)	2,000.00	9,000.0
1937	2.00	35.00
1948	20.00	90.00
CANADIAN SILVER DOLLAR		
1935	15.00	50.00
1937	9.00	30.00
1939	7.00	25.00
1947 (maple leaf)	90.00	200.00
1948	175.00	325.00
1949	10.00	25.00
1958 (Totem Pole)	3.00	9.00
CANADIAN GOLD		
$5		
1912	60.00	100.00
1913	65.00	110.00
1914	250.00	400.00
$10		
1912	150.00	225.00
1913	175.00	300.00
1914	225.00	350.00

Sovereigns

The Canadian Sovereign with the mintmark "C" was struck at the Ottawa Mint.

	Good	Unc.
1908 (C)	500.00	850.00
1911 (C)	20.00	35.00
1919 (C)	27.50	40.00

NEWFOUNDLAND

The coinage of Newfoundland is now included in all books listing Canadian coins. The last year the Newfoundland coins were issued was 1947 and a great many have been melted since, making almost all pieces now collectors' items.

	Good	Unc.
NEWFOUNDLAND LARGE CENT		
1865	$ 1.50	$ 37.50
1876 (Heaton Mint)	1.50	40.00
1880 (round O, even date)	2.00	40.00
1880 (round O, low date)	1.50	42.50
1880 (oval O)	45.00	225.00
1888	10.00	65.00
1917 (C)	.30	12.50
NEWFOUNDLAND SMALL CENT		
1938	.75	15.00
1940	3.00	30.00
1947 (C)	.75	12.50
NEWFOUNDLAND 5¢ SILVER		
1865	12.50	125.00
1872 (Heaton)	12.00	155.00
1880	15.00	200.00
1917 (C)	1.50	40.00
1946 (C, only 2,041 issued)	200.00	300.00
1947 (C)	9.00	27.50
NEWFOUNDLAND 10¢		
1865	7.50	125.00
1872 (Heaton)	4.50	125.00
1880	15.00	250.00
1903	1,25	75.00
1919 (C)	1.50	75.00
1947 (C)	.60	20.00
NEWFOUNDLAND 20¢		
1865	2.50	100.00
1872 (Heaton)	3.50	125.00

	Good	Unc.
1885	$ 2.00	$ 85.00
1896 (comes with wide date and narrow date both having approximately the same value)	1.00	60.00
1904 (Heaton)	5.00	150.00
1912	.75	50.00

NEWFOUNDLAND QUARTER

This denomination was only issued for two years.

	Good	Unc.
1917 (C)	.50	22.50
1919 (C)	.75	32.50

NEWFOUNDLAND HALF-DOLLAR

	Good	Unc.
1870	4.00	225.00
1872 (Heaton)	4.00	250.00
1880	6.00	325.00
1899 (comes with narrow 9 and wide 9, both of equal value)	1.25	175.00
1907	1.25	125.00
1917 (C)	.75	55.00

NEWFOUNDLAND $2 GOLD

All of the Newfoundland gold was issued in small quantities, the largest mintage being 25,000 in 1882.

	Very Good	Unc.
1865	40.00	100.00
1870	40.00	110.00
1872	50.00	225.00
1880	100.00	600.00
1881	40.00	100.00
1882 (Heaton)	45.00	85.00
1885	50.00	110.00
1888	45.00	85.00

The Coins of Mexico

Since 1536, when the first mint was opened in Mexico, this country has issued many denominations and varieties of coins at eleven mints. The early Mexican coins, or Spanish Colonials, as they are often referred to, with the pieces of eight, doubloons, etc., have a real romance to them and are collected over the entire world. In recent years, collecting of modern Mexican numismatic material has skyrocketed.

This is a short, representative listing of some of the various types, varieties and dates and prices are averaged from various catalogs and auctions. Top grades of early Mexican coinage are very difficult to obtain.

LARGE COPPER CENTAVO

1870 (Mexico Mint)	VERY FINE	$ 9.00
1887 (Mexico Mint)	EXTREMELY FINE	1.75
1889 (Mexico Mint)	UNCIRCULATED	8.00
1890 (Ga. Mint)	GOOD	2.00
1891 (Mexico Mint)	UNCIRCULATED	7.50
1897 (Mexico Mint)	EXTRA FINE	2.50
1898 (Mexico Mint) restyled eagle	VERY FINE	7.50

SMALL CENTAVO

	Good	Very Fine
1920	$ 2.00	$ 9.50
1928	.25	2.25
1929	.25	1.75
1935	.05	.35

TWO CENTAVOS

1905 Bronze	6.00	30.00
1915, reduced size	2.50	10.00
1920	.40	2.75
1929	2.75	15.00

	Good	Very Fine
FIVE CENTAVOS, NICKEL		
1905	$ .35	$ 3.75
1912	5.00	30.00
FIVE CENTAVOS, BRONZE		
1914	.25	1.50
1924	1.00	6.50
TEN CENTAVOS		
1864 (Potosi, Emperor Maximilian)	7.50	30.00
1905	.50	1.75
1921	1.00	6.00

	Good	Unc.
TWENTY CENTAVOS		
1905 (Mexico)	.75	8.50
1907 (comes with straight 7 and curved 7, both of equal value)	.50	7.50
1919	5.00	50.00
1920 (large size bronze)	1.00	12.50
1927	.35	5.00
FIFTY CENTAVOS		
1866 (Emperor Maximilian)	12.50	75.00
1908	1.50	25.00
PESOS		
1866 (Emperor Maximilian)	12.50	60.00
1902 (Zacatecas) Cap and rays	2.50	6.50
1910 (Caballito)	2.75	12.00
1918	2.00	22.50
1938	.75	2.00
8 REALES		
1860, Cn	7.00	30.00
1863, Do	4.00	20.00
1872, As	8.75	75.00
1879, Go	2.75	6.00
1880, Ga	4.00	20.00
1881 (Alamos)	5.00	35.00

	Good	Unc.
1891 (Mexico)	$ 2.50	$ 7.50

5 PESOS, SILVER

1950 Railroad		12.00
1953 Hidalgo		2.50
1959 Carranza		2.00

25 PESOS

1968 Olympic		2.75

The coins of Great Britain, Australia, New Zealand, and British Colonies are now being collected by dates and mintmarks. It is only a question of time until Central America, South America, and all other countries of the world will be collected on the same basis. The main factor in this new trend is the publication of new books and catalogs with hitherto unpublished mintages and other pertinent information to aid the collector.

New coin holders, with appropriate setups, simplify assembling the material, for both beginning and advanced collector.

Please remember that my listing and pricing of the coins of the United States, Canada, and Mexico, is just a skeleton listing in order to assist in approximating the values in certain areas. You may want to acquire some of the excellent reference volumes available to assist in buying or selling when your collection increases in size, complexity or completeness.

The listings above will best help determine whether an item is common or scarce. Beyond that, condition is very important in determining what the premium on a particular coin would be, and must be considered along with mintage, popularity, and demand.

XIII

∎

Coins of Israel

Coins of Israel are among the most discussed and collected items today in the foreign field. Not only are they sought after by collectors, but by investors, who have followed the trend of this country's coinage.

Israel is a country only twenty years old and both the stamps and coins have been extremely popular with collectors.

The Israeli Government, through its Israel Government Coins & Medals Corporation, Ltd., has endeavored to supply not only coins of fine workmanship, but suitable information and has even obtained advice from numismatists of their own country to produce items which would appeal to local collectors, as well as those throughout the world. Slowly but surely there has been a steady increase in the number of Israel coin collectors and this is reflected in the large number of clubs which specialize in Israeli material only.

The first coin club of this nature to be founded was the Israel Coin Club of Los Angeles three years ago under leadership of Benjamin Abelson, well known collector in the Southern California area. Now new clubs are forming all over North America, including Montreal, San Francisco, Chicago, Washington, D. C. There is also a national organization called The American Israel Numismatic Organization with headquarters in New York, which in a comparatively short period has more than 2,000 members.

There are a number of excellent Israel numismatic books—"The History of Modern Israel's Money" by Sylvia Haffner; and the catalog of "Israel's 20 Years of Coin and Currency" by Fred Bertram and Robert Weber.

The annual Mint or Specimen Sets have been issued since 1963, with the one exception being the year 1964. The demand for these has been enormous, one example being the 1965 Specimen Sets, with 156,000 sets minted, sold out in one day and due to the unprecedented demand. The Israel government refunded over $1 million in over subscriptions. The 1963 and 1965 Specimen Sets should be good investments for the years to come. The 1965 sets are popular as they include a number of "key" coins which have low mintages.

The commemorative coins of Israel have been extremely popular during the past few years and have attracted a great many collectors as well as investors. The government officially melted some of these which were in their vaults and of course the remainder have been in great demand.

Israel first issued commemorative coins in 1958, with a 10th anniversary Independence Day coin. A coin in the Independence Day series has been issued each year to date, usually in 5-pound denomination and in .900 silver. In 1968 a 10-pound silver, also .900, was issued.

1968 Israel First Day-First Issue Cover

Another group is called the Chanukah series, which was issued from 1958 through 1963. There are two items in the Purim series, issued in 1961 and 1962, and there is a Victory commemorative, 1967, 10-pound piece. There are a number of gold commemoratives, most of them with low mintages.

Most of the commemoratives are of great beauty and fit into the Crown class; Crowns, called Dollar Size coins, have long been popular as a type of collecting among numismatists.

There are a few commemoratives which have a potential to the investor. The 1959 Ingathering, which had almost three-fourths of its issue melted and less than 30 thousand remaining; the 1964 Museum piece in Proof condition, with only 4,500 pieces minted is also an item to be reckoned with. The 1967 Eilat is an item that has received a great deal of publicity since the Israel-Arab war and has had a wide distribution throughout the world.

Trade Coins

Israel uses the term "trade coins" for the regular coins

made for general circulation. The Israel Numismatic Society assisted the Provisional Government with suggestions and designs. Their coins bear symbols taken from the ancient and biblical Jewish coinage and have proved extremely popular among collectors. Some collectors try to match up ancient coins with the same symbols as the modern ones, making for an interesting and historical collection or exhibit.

The first coins struck were in aluminum of 25 mils denomination and were produced in 1948. In 1949, 25 mils were again minted, along with other denominations called the "pruta" coins. In 1960, a new series of coins were produced and were called the "agora" coins.

On the whole, the mintages of Israel coins are small in comparison with those of other countries.

There is a new concept in hobby collecting called "First day-First issue" covers, which combines philately and numismatics. Recently covers were produced for the first time for Israel and these met with the most gratifying response in the collector world. When the Israel government heard of the new hobby they were most enthusiastic and both stamp and coin divisions of the government cooperated fully. As a result, 1,050 sets of covers were produced for Israel, dated on the first day of issue of the new Israel 1968 Specimen coin sets, February 20, 1968.

With the help of the government, beautiful stamps were selected. Included in this series was a 15 agorot, showing the Symbol of Victory with attached tab "Be strong and of good courage"; a 12 and 15 agorot with ancient Scrolls of the Law on gold and silver backgrounds; a 12 and 18 agorot with native animals; and a 15 agorot commemorating the tenth anniversary of the Balfour Declaration with a portrait of Dr.

1969 Israel Specimen Set

Chaim Weizmann. The covers were postmarked in Jerusalem.

The coins in the six covers are the 50 agorot, 25 agorot, 10 agorot, 5 agorot, one agora and the one pound. The coins used were all taken from the Israel 1967 Specimen Sets.

The astounding demand for these covers triggered a complete sellout in a few days. These covers are produced by the 99 Company of Capistrano Beach, California, who will issue other Israel covers in 1969 and the years to come.

A Star of David appears in the panel area on the obverse of the cover, making it an unusual and beautiful collector's item, and the postmarks are excellently done as they were prepared by the government in Jerusalem.

This new hobby is one which bears watching!

The State Medals of Israel are actually wonderful works of art and most of them have been designed by Israelis. The first, the Rothschild medal issued in 1966, and the Balfour Declaration Medal issued in 1967 were designed by Paul Vincze, and were well received all over the world.

One group of medals provides an introduction to the City coins of ancient Israel, as each one bears a replica of an ancient coin connected with the site of a modern city, while the reverse symbolizes a familiar aspect of the city as it is today.

Medallic art has become extremely popular in recent years and is moving ahead at a rapid pace.

Of added note is the interest in the coins of Palestine, which were issued from 1927 through 1947. The word "Palestine" appears on all coins in three languages—Hebrew, English and Arabic, and are collected in addition to the Israeli series.

The profit derived from the sale of coins by the Israel Government Coins & Medals Corporation, Ltd. is used for archeological expeditions and studies.